Create Your Own Career
In Hollywood

Advice from a Struggling Actress
Who Became a Successful Producer

Create Your Own Career in Hollywood:
Advice from a Struggling Actress Who Became a Successful
Producer

© 2017 by Alexandra Boylan

All articles except for "Rising Together" originally published on
Ms In the Biz, www.msinthebiz.com

Cover design by Dog & Pony Creative
Book editing by Renee Wurzer and Barbara Hethcock
Articles arranged by Ashley Serrao
Formatting by Polgarus Studio

Printed in the United States of America

ISBN: 978-0-9995305-0-4 (print)
ISBN: 978-0-9995305-1-1 (kindle)
ISBN: 978-0-9995305-2-8 (epub)
Library of Congress Control Number: 2017918525

"Special Thanks to Helenna Santos for creating Ms. In The Biz, which gives women a platform for their voices to be heard. It helped me to find mine!"

Contents

THE MINDFUL CREATIVE

1. Be Yourself. Be "Youer Than You"!

There is a temptation in life to try to be someone else, to conform to the masses, to people please, or change in order to be liked, especially in the film industry.

I was nineteen when I moved to Los Angeles, and my first week out here I got an audition for a music video. I was so excited as I drove to that first LA audition, parking my car and hustling up to the door, I remember it like it was yesterday. I sat down across from the director and he explained a little about the music video, and the "bitchy" character he was casting. I sat there listening, intently nodding my head. Then he said, "So are you a bitch?" I was taken off guard with this question, and hesitated saying, "No, I'm not, but I can act like a bitch." He then said, "Well do you get aggravated easily, do you fly off the handle and get pissed off easily?" I replied again shaking my head "No actually I don't, but I can act like I do." The director stood up and went to the door, he opened it smiled and said,

"Thank you." I grabbed my bag and headed out the door. As I walked to my car I thought, "Wow, I just blew that audition." I was thinking the whole drive home, "Man I should have just said I was a bitch." I spent the rest of the afternoon kicking myself.

A few hours later the director called me and said "You booked the role. You were the only girl who told me the truth. Everyone else just told me what they thought I wanted to hear, that they were a 'bitch' I liked that you were honest."

I booked that first audition in LA and it was all thanks to the fact that I wasn't jaded enough yet to know any different than to tell the truth and be honest about whom I really was.

I wish I could say that experience kept me from becoming a person who would conform or change in order to be who I thought people wanted me to be. Sadly I still got caught up in the game of wanting to be liked, trying to be the right type, even if I was grasping at straws as to what "right" was.

As an actor it was easy to get desperate, and want so badly to be chosen that I would constantly be running like a hamster in a wheel trying to figure out how to please the people in the film industry.

I remember a good friend once telling me that I was too nice and that could be the reason I wasn't booking jobs. Casting directors might have thought I was being fake. So I started trying to figure out how not to be myself, which is a super happy, bubbly girl with a lot of enthusiasm and energy. I think I was born with an insane amount of serotonin running through my veins. I began desperately trying to figure out how to change. I even found myself apologizing for who I was, which is an exhausting way to live.

It took me many years to finally embrace my true self, and to accept me, without anyone else's permission. I am the kind of girl whose energy is a bit crazy. I'm loud, talk really fast, and get extremely excitable and passionate about things, and that's ok 'cause if someone doesn't like it then they don't have to spend time with me. My husband says sometimes my energy is bouncing off the walls and he has to leave the room for a minute. That's who I am and I can't change, even with all those years of trying. I finally gave up the fight, and it was the most freeing feeling in the world. To be comfortable in my own skin, and to give up the desperate attempt to be someone I am not. To love and accept myself is a beautiful way to live.

I recently saw a very touching clip from the Oscars, where actresses were asked what advice they would give to young girls today, and the answers all mentioned "embracing who you are, and not trying to be someone else."

This is the best advice anyone could give someone else. I wish it hadn't taken me so long to figure it out, but now that I have, I live in a much more peaceful, pleasant place in my mind. I know that the people I surround myself with really do love me because they are seeing who I really am and not a front of whom I think they might like.

Embrace and love yourself and you will attract the people and the career that is meant to be in your life. Life is too short and precious not to exude your unique "you" into the world. And if you don't want to take my word for it, maybe you'll take it from Dr. Seuss.

"Today you are you, that is truer than true. There is no one alive who is youer than you."—Dr. Seuss

2. Definition of insanity- "Doing the same thing over and over expecting different results"

After years of practically slamming my head against walls, trying to figure out how to "work hard enough" to succeed as an actress, a light went on in my head! What if I choose myself? So after pulling out of the rat race of being a struggling actress, I jumped into becoming a successful producer. I decided I wanted control over my career, and in just a few short years, the first production company I formed was Mirror Tree Productions. I produced numerous short films, a twelve-episode web series, and a feature film (distributed by Image Entertainment). I star in each of the films. Voila- In turn I became a working actress. After finally thinking outside the box, and trying different things, I was able to make my dreams come true. Creating your own work is the key to success in the film industry! Actually it is the key to any industry!

Instead of chasing after the job you want, I say create the job you want!

3. Reconstructing Your Life

Growing up in rural Massachusetts I dreamed of becoming an actress. Starting out in my father's church, and going on to perform in all my school plays, I fell madly in love with the art of performing. As my high school years were coming to an end, I made up my mind: I was going to move to LA to convince Hollywood I was the next big STAR!

After one year of college per my parents' request, I packed up my Toyota Corolla and headed west in search of my dreams.

Nineteen years old without a single friend in that town, I began to wade through the waves of a massive ocean. I became obsessed with succeeding as an actor, so much so that I gave up every other talent I had possessed.

Quickly I fell into a rut and began doing the same thing over and over expecting different results. Getting a job as a waitress to support myself, running to auditions every day with desperation in my eyes, begging the casting director to pick me. Disappointment washing over me at every turn because I couldn't work hard enough for someone else to choose me.

Ten years went by before I even realized it, and I woke up one morning with a sea of emotions wondering if I was truly happy waiting for someone else to hand me my dreams. Was I willing to wait another ten years for someone else to choose me? That morning it dawned on me that I could choose myself, I could start creating my own projects. It was time for me to take charge of my destiny and change the course of my story. I was done watching myself sit back as others dictated my path in life. No longer was I going to fall victim to believing that I had no control over my future.

As I struggled to find a new direction in LA, and in an attempt to break free from my old habits, I partnered with a friend to produce a play. It was the first step in taking charge of creating my future. And even though the play was a success, I still felt stuck in LA with an empty heart. Something was missing and I couldn't quite put my finger on what it was. I felt like it was time for a change.

Within a month I lost my job and apartment, and felt fully convicted that it was a sign for me to move. I packed my bags yet again, ten years from the date I had so bravely arrived in the City of Lights, I watched as they grew dim in the rear view mirror, the highway stretched before me. And to my amazing surprise I felt myself crumbling in the best way. Freedom washed over me, and a new hope was on the horizon.

Albuquerque, New Mexico was the new Hollywood. I heard it "buzz" throughout my community, and I believed if I could just start over in a new place with a new outlook I could do great things. And boy was I right. First I let go of all my old ways of thinking. I even got a totally different job. I became a companion to elderly people, and spent a lot of time alone reflecting on my past choices and envisioning my new ones. My heart was open to whatever I was meant to do with my life: letting go of my own desires and releasing my grip on my previous way of thinking.

Once I did that I got my life back tenfold. I quickly tapped into the filmmaking community in New Mexico and began meeting like-minded people who wanted to create projects with me. I even met my husband on a set of a short film. My dream of having a partner in life and a partner in creating came true. Just a few short years after turning my life upside down I became the owner of two production companies, my life full and rich, while I was making my own dreams come true. No longer waiting for other people to pick me, I was able to pick myself and I have never looked back.

For me feeling stuck in life was the most devastating emotion. It led me into a downward spiral of depression and hopelessness. If I feel this way, I'm sure there are millions of other women out there struggling with this same path. The incredible truth is that we have the power and ability to change our circumstances at any time, even if that means moving out of our comfort zone to experience a new rich way of living. Jumping into the unknown can be daunting but if you are unhappy, the only person that can change it is you. There is no time like the present to make the adjustments that will secure the future of your heart's desire. We have but one precious life, why spend it doing anything we despise or dread? It is never too late to take the leap of faith, and begin again in a new way. Every morning is a new day, and a new chance to go after the things you have always wanted. And if you fail, who cares? Get up and try again.

Sometimes in order to construct the life you have always dreamed of, you must deconstruct the old one.

4. Ignoring the Negative Noise

It was recently brought to my attention that there was a podcast called "God Awful Movies" (really that's the name of their podcast). For an hour and a half two men review a Christian movie and completely rip it to shreds.

Now, I'm not sure what is worse about this podcast, the fact that these people have dedicated their lives to making fun of Christians, or making fun of people's hard work creating a movie. Nonetheless, this podcast spent an hour and thirty-eight minutes to go through my film "Catching Faith" and rip it apart scene by scene.

I probably shouldn't have listened to this podcast, but it started out kind of funny, and I was able to laugh along with it until it got out of hand, and they personally attacked the people involved in this film including me.

It took me a couple of days to shake the insults these men spewed out, and then I realized, I should take it as the highest form of a compliment that they spent such a long time discussing my film. I mean, isn't that actually a form of flattery?

Either way, I know I cannot please everyone with my films, and I have gotten really good at ignoring the negative noise that comes when you are willing to put your work out there. I suggest you do the same, don't make a film to impress someone else, make something that impresses you.

My advice for filmmakers is to grow thick skin, because freedom of speech is a good thing, and when we put our work out there, we must be willing to receive the "hate" that comes along with the "love." There is no such thing as a "perfect" movie, although some people have tried to convince me there is (these people have never actually made a movie, mind you) and art is subjective. If you went around a room and asked everyone what was "good" each person would give a different answer.

The alternative is to hold on tight to your "work" and never put it out there for fear of rejection or criticism. As Seth Godin often says in his blogs, you must "ship it." You must at some point say, ok this is good enough, let it go, send it out there and move on to the next project. And if you are afraid of the negative noise, then don't look up reviews on your films, which is a simple way to avoid it.

At the end of the day, be brave, create what you love, and ignore the people who "love" to "hate" other people's hard work. I bet most of the negative comments that are left on reviews for films are from people who have never made a movie. It is so easy to hide behind a computer screen and spend an hour "bashing" on someone else's hard work. That's easy; the hard thing is putting two years of your life into creating a piece of cinema!

So know that if you are making movies, you are the small percentage of people who are actually doing "it." Pat yourself on the back, heck give yourself a HUGE hug. You are AMAZING!

If this were easy everyone would do it!

"Critics should find meaningful work." John Grisham

5. The Technology Loop

Have you ever felt like you are trapped in a never-ending technology loop? Well if you are anything like me then you know the feeling of drowning in your own devices. I once watched an episode of "Portlandia" and thought "WOW, I guess I'm not alone in this world." It's been over a year since I saw the episode, and only now am I really realizing how trapped I truly have become, and how ready I am to change.

The question is how do we balance our lives with an existence that is surrounded by computers, smart phones, tablets, and the loop that just doesn't stop? I have been ruminating over this for many weeks now. Knee deep in pre-production for my feature film "Catching Faith", I feel myself melting into a deep pool of quick sand, unable to find a way to come up for air (literally sometimes I forget to breathe, and I find myself taking huge inhales). There is always one more thing to do, one more email to answer, text to address, tweet to send, Facebook update to read and the loop goes on forever.

I recently picked up a copy of Arianna Huffington's book, "Thrive", thinking it was about female domination in the work place, but to my surprise it was all about how to find peace. Balance between being a workaholic and enjoying the simple pleasures of a life filled with love, friends and family. A few pages into the book I felt like I should stand up in a room filled with my peers and state, "Hello, my name is Alexandra Boylan and I am a workaholic!" This book couldn't have come into my life at a more perfect time. I find myself grouchy, cranky, burnt out, snapping at my husband, and feeling overwhelmed constantly, with no idea how to escape myself and my insane need to never stop. When my husband and I started producing our own projects, and I can honestly say we haven't taken a day off since. We sometimes worked until three in the morning, because if we spent one more hour on it, that's one more hour faster it will be done, and that many more steps closer to a finished project.

When you don't clock in and out of a job, it's hard to find your own boundaries and give yourself permission to stop for the day. I have heard some people can't work from home because they lack the discipline to stay on track without someone telling them what to do. Well I have found my husband and I are the opposite, we NEVER stop working because no one has given us permission to go home for the day. How do you go home, when your office is your home? It has led us into a very unhealthy existence and this wakeup call is not being ignored. My husband and I often joke around about how much gray hair we acquired since forming our first production company, but I'm starting to think "What's funny about that?" If we don't find a way to change, we might send ourselves into an early grave.

In the year 2009, I moved from Los Angeles, CA to Albuquerque, NM to escape the grind of a city that never sleeps. I knew the moment my car was outside of LA that I needed a break from the hustle and bustle, and the never-ending rat race of trying to succeed. Upon my arrival I decided to seek out a job that had nothing to do with myself. I wanted to have a job with meaning, something that I could be proud of. I wanted to focus on others, rather than myself. I was hired for a company called "Home Instead Senior Care" and I began a journey that would change my life. I became a companion to elderly people, and I flourished in my quiet moments with people who had lived extraordinary lives. My job was to listen to them, love them, and make them feel special as they moved into the final years, months, weeks, even days of their lives. I was hired to bring joy to these people, but really they brought joy to me. I remember vividly entering one elderly gentleman's home; I was led through halls lined with plaques, medals, and awards for his involvement with NASA. This man had done remarkable things, and the proof was encased in glass surrounding him. When I sat down I inquired about his life achievements, and he quickly waved his hand discarding everything I had just seen, and started telling me about his family, his wife, and the years he had shared with her before she passed away. I sat there deeply moved by his words of appreciation and admiration for her and the home they had built together. This man was not the only client I worked with that had walls of accomplishments or outstanding life achievements. The one thing they all had in common was that at the end of their time here on earth, as they sat with a stranger, all they wanted to share with me was the stories of their family. No one wanted to talk about his or her jobs; they only wanted to reflect on the family they had created! Their pride was in their loved ones, not the shinny medals hanging on the walls.

This job gave me first hand insight to what really is important at the end of our lives, and yet here I am only a few short years past those days, and I am back to being a career obsessed woman. How quickly I forgot the importance of taking time to stop and appreciate the people in my life, to turn my devices off and sit face to face with a real live human being, listening to what they have to say, getting to know them without the constant buzzing of my phone pulling my attention away.

I spent a month on eighteen acres of land in the middle of nowhere New Mexico, and even in the quiet of the desert I couldn't find peace, because I could not stop being addicted to technology. I would go for a walk, and find my mind was still on an e-mail I knew I had to respond to, or I would rush through my afternoon stroll attending to the constant blinking light of my iPhone text messages. I had convinced myself that I MUST answer everything immediately, and my patience was wearing thin. A few weeks into my time on the mountain, I really started taking notice of my unhealthy behavior. With a desperate need in my heart to relax, I stopped taking my phone on my walks, even if it meant I couldn't listen to my iTunes library. I started turning my devices off at dinnertime, and forced myself not to check my email until the next morning. I was giving my devices more attention than my mental health, and that is not good for my inner being or my business.

One big step I am taking in curing myself of being a technology looped addict is I now take Sundays off! I turn my computer off on Saturday night and I do not allow myself to open it until Monday morning. I only allow myself to text message with my family on Sunday, otherwise I call it a technology free day, and I have found that with this true day off, I feel recharged, and rejuvenated to start my week of work. It is possible to work yourself into the ground, and I believe our work suffers when we don't give ourselves the much-needed time off, so our minds can become clear and our body can recover from the non-stop noise.

I am yet to be cured of my addiction, but I believe taking the time to recognize it, puts me on the right track to recovery.

One of my brothers is also a workaholic. I used to think his love for surfing and paddle boarding was just a hobby, but I have realized it's the only time in his crazy business-filled days where he can get away from his devices. What a perfect place to leave it all behind. The ocean, it forces you to leave it all on the sand or it will be destroyed by the water.

And don't forget-be present because you will never be here again!

6. There Is No Such Thing as a Quick Fix

We live in a quick fix society, a one-minute video viewing world. As the Internet has grown at massive speeds of light, our attention span has shrunk to a minimum. I know this from making on-line content, the shorter the better, because people are already on to the next thing before they even really process the first. I have been a victim to this mentality, and it crippled my ability to accomplish anything for a long time.

Many, many years ago when I was fervently racing after a career as an actress, I had so many ideas of things I wanted to do beyond just acting. But I would stop myself in my tracks thinking of how much time something might take. Even my desire to go back to school and get my degree just seemed too daunting, three years felt like a million and I just didn't think I had the time. I wanted to start creating my own projects, write a book, and so forth, but got so caught up in the worry of time, that I never did anything.

Then as the years went by, I realized wow, if I had started that project or had gone back to school it would be done by now. And that moment when the light bulb went off in my head changed my mentality for good! I decided I wanted to change the course of my life and begin accomplishing things I was proud of, so when the next two years had gone by I wouldn't be sitting around wishing I had done something. I would be happy I accomplished something worthwhile. Out of this realization became my career as a producer/writer/actor/entrepreneur/artist/lover of life. I felt fulfilled for the first time in my life, because as the years went by I had more and more incredible accomplishments that I could be proud of. Instead of regretting my wasted time, I was proud of my time well spent.

A very clear example of my turning point that helped change my mentality was in the year 2005 when I developed acid reflux disease. Not able to fly to Boston, MA to visit my holistic doctor, I spent WAY too much money to see a doctor in Los Angeles, CA. Upon my visit he didn't even examine my body, he just prescribed me with the purple pill. Which I was well aware that the drug only masks the problem but doesn't heal it. I walked out of his room furious, a couple hundred dollars poorer, and no solution closer to a cure.

I started doing research, and began a slow, patient process of healing myself drug free. I talked to my holistic doctor in

Massachusetts and a few other holistic healers, and learned all I could about what acid reflux disease. In case you're wondering, it is when your stomach has moved up into your rib cage, and it literally needs to be repositioned. So I would lie on the floor with my knees up, taking three deep breaths into my abdomen, on the fourth breath (holding it) I would place my thumb in between my ribs and push my stomach down as I exhaled. I could feel and hear my stomach releasing back to where it belonged. Repeating this procedure a few more times, I felt complete relief. I started frequently giving myself these "treatments" whenever I had an attack. In addition to "treatments" I became very aware of what I was eating, to figure out what was causing the problem. I had to change my diet, and remove the things that gave me attacks. I temporarily stopped drinking coffee, and alcohol, and eating fried food, until my body was healed and able to handle them again. Over time I began to have fewer and fewer acid reflux attacks, and eventually I had none.

This process took me a full year, and it was life changing for me. This experience taught me discipline; my body was worth the time it took to heal without further harm from pharmaceuticals that just masked the symptoms. This in turn awakened me to the realization that my future needed the same kind of attention. My future was worth putting in the time it would need to create a better life for myself.

There is no such thing as a quick fix, and anything worth doing is going to take time and discipline. As we fight against a rapidly accelerating environment of "give it to me now", "tell me faster", "do it quicker", we must learn the art of patience once again. It's okay to slow down, take some time to think and cultivate your thought process, get your bearings and begin.

Life is a marathon not a sprint, and what you start today will come to fruition tomorrow. As I have learned in my life experiences, first you have to get in the race at the starting line!

7. Don't Listen to Naysayers

When I first moved to LA, many moons ago, I had a meeting with a producer at Warner Brothers. His advice to me as a young fresh off-the-boat actress was to never do extra work or ever be seen as anything but an actor. I took his advice to heart, and went into my tunnel of going at this industry in one direction: waiting tables slash waiting for people to pick me to audition for their films. This man generously gave me three days as an extra on his show to obtain my Screen Actors Guild Union card and looking back at this experience, I recall being invited along with a couple other extras to go to a party with the cast and crew. I got to meet a ton of industry people that night, and still after those three days were up, I never did extra work again. I don't know about you, but I feel pretty dumb for making that choice. I was just too young to realize how important it was to meet people, even if it was through an avenue that wasn't being an actor.

I look back with fury at myself for listening to such directionless advice. I have since learned that the worst thing anyone in the film industry can do, is to NOT be on set.

Flash-forward ten years later, I packed my bags, and moved to Albuquerque, NM with a new fresh perspective of being OPEN to any opportunities that came my way. One of these was to be Megan Fox's stand in on a film called "Passion Play." I booked the job, and embarked on one of my favorite life experiences to this day. Being on set was a pure joy, and I felt blessed to be treated so well by the director and the rest of the crew. In fact on one of the weekends, a bunch of the crew and I shot a "Wonder Woman" short. By putting myself on set I was able to do what I really wanted, which was acting.

Almost a year later, I received a phone call from the post production coordinator of "Passion Play" and was asked to come in to read for the lead role in the producers cut of the film. I landed the part, and went on to work with some incredible names in this industry, and all because I had been a "stand in" on the film. The footage never saw the light of day, but the connections I made were priceless. I continue to work with the crew on different projects, and cherish that character I got to play as an actor. No experience is a waste of time; every path leads to new opportunities.

And to think someone told me not to be on set as anything but an actor!

The film industry is changing, and I believe the best way in, is to go around the back door. Find any way to be on set, to meet hard working, driven people, and align yourself with those folks. Find people who inspire you, and instead of envying them, learn from them. Success rises in groups, so find people who are heading in the direction you want.

So many people want to tell others not to do something, or that something isn't possible. I once heard that if Steve Jobs asked someone to do something and they said, "that's not possible" he would fire them, and find someone who could make it possible. What an incredible outlook on life, to never believe anything is impossible. When our team was creating the app game, so many people said technology wasn't ready for our idea, but we created programming that could house the invention. I'm so thankful that we didn't listen to any of this negative advice, and we just charged ahead. Today we ARE beta testing that game, and our idea has become a reality. All because a group of people gathered together and said "What if?" Then we turned that question into an answer.

There are so many things I wish I could go back and tell my younger self, but since time travel hasn't been invented yet, I just keep reminding myself to be open minded. To never say no to an opportunity, even if it might not be my ultimate goal, it might just be the back door entrance to the dream destination!

There will always be naysayers out there telling you that something can't or shouldn't be done and it might be true, there are no guarantees; but ONE guarantee is it is definitely impossible if you don't try! In show business there is only one rule, and that is that there are NO rules!

8. Hello, My Name is Alexandra, and I am Addicted to "Stress."

In the past month I have noticed and recognized that I am completely addicted to the feeling of being "stressed out." I actually love the rush it gives me, so when I don't feel it, I feel like something is wrong with me.

I have spent most of my life stressed out about something, whether it was money or a job or my relationships. The feeling of being "stressed out" is so familiar to me that I recently started stressing about not being stressing out

Sound crazy? Well, you're right. It is and I am ready to stop the crazy!

According to Dictionary.com "stress" has a couple of meanings:

Stress – *special emphasis or significance attached to something*

Stress – *mental, emotional, or physical strain or tension.*

Now, when the first definition is put into practice it is a good thing, and I will say my stress has led me to never give up and accomplish what I put my mind to. When under stress I work furiously to finish the task at hand. The adrenaline and high makes me motivated to get sh** done!

I also struggle with the second definition, and the problem is, I think I like it. Your body releases chemicals like dopamine or adrenaline when triggered by certain activities or emotions. I think my brain and body are addicted to the chemical release caused by "stress."

I sold my second feature film "Catching Faith" and am in the writing room on my next one. I haven't had to strap on a waitressing apron in almost a year now, and I currently don't have any financial issues. The career I have spent years trying to build is finally falling into place, my life is where I have always wanted it to be, but I have discovered I can't relax or enjoy it. I WANT to stress out about something. It's my "go to" emotion and without it I feel empty, like a drug addict who will find any way to get their hands on that little pill.

The other day I watched Marie Forleo's video "Upper Limits" and the light went on in my head. I had just picked a fight with my husband (for no reason at all by the way), the night before watching this video. After my very patient husband listened to my tirade, I sat down on the couch and wondered what the heck was wrong with me. Thank God for Marie's video, which explains "upper limits" so well, and gave me the tools to recognize what was causing my behavior and frustration.

I am moving onward and upward in my career and finally getting to live the life I have always dreamed of. In turn, I don't have anything to "stress" out about, at the moment, so I find things to "stress" out about. This is how my "upper level" starts kicking in. Some people withdraw, some get sick, some self–sabotage, ME-I find a reason to be "stressed" out.

When I realized I had this addiction, I wondered how many other people out there might be struggling with it too, and thought here would be a great place to start a dialogue about it. Just like being "busy" is a sickness, so is being "stressed out." I can't even express how much I crave the rush and must have that feeling. When it's vacant from my life I start feeling out of control. Now that I recognize this, I want to find a way to conquer it. I want to be able to relax and enjoy my peaceful existence as a working filmmaker.

I don't have the answers to the questions yet, but recognition is always the first step to recovery.

I would love to hear your thoughts, guidance, tools and tips on managing a "stress" addiction.

Hello my name is Alexandra and I am addicted to STRESS.

9. What's "Worth It" to You?

In the fall of 1999 I packed up my Toyota Corolla and headed out west to follow my dreams! I was nineteen years old, full of hope and promise, determined to live a life I loved. It was worth it to me, to move three thousand miles away from everything I knew to pursue everything I wanted. By summer of 2000 I found myself homeless. Living in my car, determined not to give up, I stuck it out. It was worth it to me to be homeless and continue forth on my journey in life. This was just the beginning of learning to make sacrifices in order to live out the life I had dreamed of.

What is "worth it" to you?

Is being an Artist/Entrepreneur

- Worth being homeless?
- Worth working overnight jobs so that you have your days free to create?
- Worth using all the money you make to produce projects you believe in?

- Worth turning your home into office spaces?
- Worth giving up luxuries to finance making your visions come to life?

These are just a few of the sacrifices I have chosen to make in order to create. When I ask myself if it was worth it, the answer is always "yes".

This subject is particularly close to my heart at the moment, because my husband and business partner John and I have decided to give up our beautiful rent controlled apartment in Los Angeles in order to make another movie. We can't financially afford both, and something had to give. Our love for filmmaking won in the end, and we are now preparing to live with my sister's family as we write the script, and go into pre-production. There are moments in your life, when you have to say 'it's now or never'. You get one life, and I believe you regret more the things you don't do, than the things you do. Regret is wasted energy, if you want something you have to "Just Do It". There is never a perfect moment to jump off the cliff into the unknown. This goes for any endeavor in life, whether you want to open up your own bookstore, coffee shop, start an on-line business, or go back to school. If it's worth it to you, you must find a way to do it.

For the past four years John and I have made many sacrifices that were "worth it" for us to make our projects. Recently someone asked me how we got funding for "Home Sweet Home", and the answer is-we make solid financial plans in advance to fund our films. We'd take a job, save the money, and when that job ended, we used that money to create our own films. Besides the money we raised on Kickstarter, John and I took all of our savings account and poured it into that movie. We couldn't work our side jobs while on location for 28 days, so we had to live off and use our savings for that movie-double whammy. The whole cast and crew took a risk by giving up work to relocate to the middle of nowhere to be a part of that film. On one of our last days of shooting our cinematographer received three phones calls to work on large budget projects and he turned them all down. First it was "In Plain Sight" then "Breaking Bad" and finally the "Avengers", literally the jobs just got bigger and bigger, and Rick continued to say no. Amazed at his dedication to our movie, I realized this was "worth it" to him.

After completion of principle photography on the film, John and I packed our bags and moved from Albuquerque to Los Angeles, in hopes of selling the movie, and moving forward with our careers. I took a waitressing job and supported him while he edited the movie. It was "worth it" to me to take a job I despised in order to give John the full time job of editing.

When we began the process of creating our live action app game "your pizza adventure", John Graham, Raquel Cantu, Andrew Miorano and myself all sat down in my apartment and decided to take a giant leap of faith to embark on that project. Two of our team members decided to hold off on getting survival jobs and used their savings account to make the app their full time job. It was a risk, and the outcome is still unknown, but it was 'worth it' to all of us to give up our lives and jobs for a year and dedicate everything to make sure that game came to completion. John and I turned our dining room into an office space and for four months the team would gather there to edit the app. By turning our living space into a workspace we forfeited having a home that was a sanctuary, but it was "worth it" to us.

I believe many stories get whittled down to overnight successes, but I guarantee you most success stories are anything but that!

The creator of Amazon.com, Jeff Bezos, decided he wanted to get involved with the internet boom in 1994, and create an online bookstore. With the support of his wife, he quit a well-paying job in NYC. From there the couple flew to Texas, were gifted a car, that Jeff's wife drove, while he typed a business plan. Once in Seattle they set up shop in a rented two-bedroom house, with extension cords running to the garage. Jeff set up three Sun Micro stations on tables he made out of doors from Home Depot for less than $60 each. On July 16th, 1995, Bezos opened his site to the world. By September it had sales of $20,000 a week. **

Steve Jobs, attended Reed College, which his parents couldn't afford so he continued auditing classes at Reed while sleeping on the floor in friends' dorm rooms, returning

Coke bottles for food money, and getting weekly free meals at the local Hare Krishna Temple. Auditing means he didn't get certified credit for those classes. In 1976 a man named Wozniak single-handedly invented the Apple I computer. He showed it to Jobs, who suggested that they sell it. The two teamed up with Ronald Wayne and together they all formed Apple Computer in the garage of Job's parents in order to sell it. *

From the outside greatness appears unreachable, but in truth, greatness might just be waiting to be discovered in your basement.

I have never been a big fan of the book "The Secret"; I do not believe you can will something into existence with your mind. Hard work and follow through is the way to will something to happen. Although you must have a positive attitude and the mindset that if you set out to do something you can accomplish it!

I was recently offered a stand in job on a show in my hometown of Massachusetts. Standing in is the furthest thing from my dream job, but it pays well and I love to be on set. So I relocated my life to this area for a few months with a very specific goal in mind; to save all the money I make and use it to support us and help fund our next feature film. But one important factor in this strategy is to NOT get sucked-in by the money, crew jobs pay well, and before you know it years have gone by and you find yourself making other people's vision come to life. About two years ago, at the exact same time we were about to start shooting our app game, I got an offer to stand in on the last season of "Breaking Bad." Trust me it was so tempting to work on one of my favorite shows, and the money was extremely appealing as I was slaving away at a restaurant job, feeling miserable. But after a long pep talk with myself, I turned down the job, and chose to continue forth with my team on the app game. I believe you have to make very strategic decisions when dealing with survival jobs versus your creation jobs.

Do you want to create your own projects? Then you have to set aside the time to DO those things. If it's "worth it" you will do it.

Spend time with people who uplift you, not tear you down. Being supported is another key element in being able to do what is "worth it" in your life. I have surrounded myself with "Yes" people, we all agree what we are doing is "worth it."

What's "Worth It" to you? Do you have a story where you made huge sacrifices to secure your dream outcome in life? If what you're doing isn't "worth it", then why continue doing it? Stop-reevaluate-refocus and find out what is 'worth it' to you! Do it TODAY, don't wait; you only have one precious lifetime, so spend it wisely!

Source from http://en.wikipedia.org/wiki/Steve_Jobs

**Source from:*
http://www.achievement.org/autodoc/page/bez0bio-1

10. The Company You Keep

I have been thinking a lot about the people I spend my time with lately. Ever since this subject came into my mind, everywhere I turn I keep reading articles about the fact that we ARE who we spend the most time with. I once read that we are the five people we surround ourselves with on a regular basis. And I put those thoughts into my mind, and decided to do some re-evaluating on my relationships.

For the past seven months of my life I have been on the road, living out of a suitcase, traveling from state to state, spending time with incredible friends all along the way. I just recently returned to Los Angeles where I am currently in pre-production on my next film project. Since my time is so limited and I have been gone for so long, I really have to pick and choose the people I am going to run around this crazy city to catch up with. And almost without thinking I discovered the people I want to surround my life with.

In my sister's workbook "The Elijah Project" there is an activity where you draw a circle and place your name in the center, and then you're advised to start placing the names of your family and friends around your own. You can move people in and out with arrows deciding who are safe people, and whom you should let close to your heart and who should be moved away.

This has spawned a new thinking in my life, and I have made a conscious effort to begin discerning between who gets my precious time and who doesn't.

In the film industry, I find this is a very important activity and mindset to constantly be reminded of. I am a positive, optimistic person in general, and feel drained after spending time with people who try to bring me down. I want to surround myself with go-getters and chargers, who like myself, drive their lives forward to accomplish their dreams and goals.

Who do you spend your time with? Is there someone who is constantly bringing you down, making it impossible to stay optimistic because of his or her pessimistic attitude? I challenge you to join me on the journey to surround yourself with people who lift you up, drive you forward and support your dreams. Just like "We are what we eat," "We are who we spend our time with!"

FILM INDUSTRY

11. Breaking into Show Business

Have you noticed we see the same people nominated year after year, the same faces popping up on our TV screens and on the big screen along with the same crewmembers in the rolling credits, so how does anyone break into this very select industry?

I recently opened my "Variety" magazine to find this headline staring back at me: "Breaking into a Crowd of Veterans." Which got me thinking, how do you break into an industry that is already populated with veterans and a line of people around the block desperate to be let in?

Hollywood has created a maze where only the strongest will survive. There is a paradox inherent to the industry where only people with known talent, credits or previous relationships can get a job.

Here are just some examples of the paradoxes surrounding the fortress called Hollywood.

1) You can't get an agent without credits, and you can't get credits without an agent.

2) There are more female directors now, as the Directors Guild of America site shows. But many of them face a vicious cycle: if a woman isn't hired she can't get experience, but she can't get experience if no one hires her. "I think we have to be better as an industry," said so brilliantly by Manohla Dargis in her article, "In Hollywood, It's a Men's, Men's, Men's World."

3) You can't get into the Union unless you have union days under your belt, and you can't get union days under your belt unless you are in the union.

It is a paradox. The problem with a paradox is it is an endless cycle with no entrance or exit route. **At least that is what Hollywood WANTS you to think**. The truth is there are ways to get a foothold and solid step in the right direction helps you break the barriers.

Here are my three tips for breaking in:

1) **Make your own stuff!** Simple as that! You must be creating your own content in any way you can. Make YouTube videos or write a blog. Whatever gets your name out there as an artist where people can follow your work and see what you have to offer to the world. You must showcase your work, your talent, and your capability, so this industry can become aware of you. In today's technology age there is

no excuse not to be creating your own work. And once you have that, viola there you have a credit to your name.

2) **Be the kind of person people want to work with.** When given an opportunity in LA (or whatever area you live in), don't squander it. It's a small town, be the kind of person people want to take with them to the top. Be positive. Be kind. Share that positivity with everyone around you. No one likes a naysayer. Positivity is contagious. This is a proven, scientific fact, that positive people breed positivity into their lives. You will go nowhere with a crummy negative attitude that brings down the people around you. People don't forget how you make them feel, so always make a fantastic impression. You need allies in this business to succeed; never forget the importance of rising in groups.

3) **There is no such thing as a small job.** Take any opportunity that comes your way, because you never know who you will meet, and what that job will lead to in the future. Never think you're above anything. Don't let your ego get in the way of success because you think you should be further along than you are. Remember you are not entitled to anything in this lifetime, and it's okay to take sides steps in order to move into the position you want. Take every opportunity as a chance to move into your dream job. This business has a lot of nepotism, and many have to start somewhere, grasp even the smallest opportunities, give it your all, and prove you belong.

I found this fabulous quote from "The 48 Laws of POWER" by Robert Greene: *"Law #10 says Infection; avoid the unhappy and unlucky; you can die from someone else's misery-emotional states are as infectious as diseases. The unfortunate sometimes draw misfortune on themselves; they will also draw it on you. Associate with the happy and fortunate instead!"*

One thing I can tell you is successful people don't waste their time around negative people who complain and play the victim game. There simply isn't enough time in the day for whining and grumbling. Successful people are pro-active people. And if you want to get your name in the list of exclusives, you'd better be ready to take on those three steps with a vengeance.

My advice is to get out of the line of people desperate to get in, and create your own path into the golden gates of Hollywood. Take risks, work hard, and bring your best attitude to work each day.

"Be so good they can't ignore you." — Steve Martin

12. It's a Small Town . . . Always Be Kind

The other day I found myself in a three-hour wait at the DMV. I had visited the DMV earlier in the week, only to discover I had to take a test and didn't have the time to do it that particular day. So now in the DMV, on this random Tuesday afternoon, I stood in the back of a crowded room filled with aggravated people constantly checking the time. I happened to be standing next to three gentlemen who struck up a conversation with me. I won't lie, if I was to have met these men on the street at night, I probably would have walked in the opposite direction. But feeling pretty safe in the company of over a hundred people, I engaged in conversation with them. They encouraged me not to worry about my test and that I would do fine, as I sat their flipping through the manual viciously trying to memorize a lifetime of driving in a couple of hours. We all chatted for a while and then one by one, their numbers got called and they headed into the test room.

A few minutes later one of the younger men came back to me, very excited that he had passed his test. I congratulated him and shared in his extreme excitement to pass the California driving test. Then his face grew serious and he said to me "I'm really happy I passed this test because I was just released from prison twelve days ago after serving eighteen years of a life sentence for a murder I didn't commit." WOW! Well you can only imagine my face after hearing this–complete shock. He shared that he was thirty-eight years old; he had spent most of his life in prison. Then he reached out his hand to mine and I shook it and he said, "Thank you for talking to me today and being so kind to me." He walked away from me and my jaw was on the floor, I couldn't believe he had shared his story with me and this experience really struck me to the heart. It was such a beautiful reminder of how important it is to always be kind to everyone you meet. You have no idea the day they might have had. Then my number was called, I hustled up the desk, only to discover I did not have to take the driving test. This was not a random Tuesday afternoon. I believe I was meant to be there that day to meet this man.

What does this have to do with the film industry you might ask?

My answer-EVERYTHING!

I feel this rings true in the film industry because it is extremely important to be the kind of person people enjoy working with. HUGE studios do not run Hollywood. It is run by people and the relationships we have with each other. You never know whom you are going to meet and how they might come across your path in years to come. Always treat people with kindness, and generosity, like the saying goes, "treat people as you would like to be treated". That's why you always see the same names popping up on films, these people enjoy working together and sometimes that might even beat out talent or money. I have worked in the film industry since I was seventeen years old and have always tried to keep this in mind: everyone I meet today could affect my tomorrow. Plus I really love working on films, so for the most part I feel complete joy when on a movie set. But I have watched others complain, bring down a crew and have always thought it was detrimental to their own experience and their future chances of working with those people again.

Many years ago I struck up a friendship with an assistant director named Justin Jones while I was waiting on him at a restaurant. A week later he called me and offered me a very small part on an Asylum film he was working on. The part only had two lines, but I jumped at the opportunity to get to play make believe. I only had one day on this film but lucky for me I met the director, Leigh Scott. About a month or so later I got a call from Leigh offering me one of the lead roles in his new film. I was beyond thrilled and got to go on location for a couple of days where I met friends that are still dear to me to this day. On set I met the lovely Sarah Lieving and she said to me "Did you know Leigh wrote the script with the actresses he wanted in mind?" I shook my head, thinking of course not, feeling extremely honored. Sarah said, "Leigh really liked you and wanted to work with you again." I was completely taken aback since I had only worked with him one day. While the conditions hadn't been the best I never complained and fully enjoyed the experience, always with a cheerful attitude. People want to work with someone they like, no drama, no fuss. If you're going to be on location together for awhile it is very important to have no diva's on set. This goes for men and women! No Divas Allowed!

This story resonated so deeply with me that I still think of it today. I am thankful for every opportunity that arrives and am always looking for new friends to collect along the way. Everyone is building a team and I know I am always looking for easygoing people to work with. On the set of our feature film "Home Sweet Home" we all lived together in a house and it was important for us to have a group of people that were a pleasure to be around. The movie would never have turned out as good as it did if we had not had so much fun working together. Our camaraderie translated into the film.

While John (the director/my husband) and I were embarking on the adventure of selling that feature film, we met with our potential future sales reps. Our decision to not sign any paper work before meeting them in person was because we wanted to see what kind of guys they were. It was very important to us to make sure we liked them before we put anything in writing. When we met Ryan Keller and

Jonny Look from Instrum International we immediately knew these guys were going to be our friends.

After they sold our movie at AFM to Image Entertainment, I was warned repeatedly from other filmmakers to watch out for sales reps and distribution companies. Horror stories started flooding in from different people about how their sales reps had screwed them over. John and I didn't worry. We just decided to trust in them and so far had been extremely happy with our relationship. We took them out for drinks as a thank you. And anytime we had questions they returned our emails promptly. They have proven their loyalty to us and have gone above and beyond on our behalf. One day our sales reps and I got together for breakfast to discuss our next project. Half way through our chat, I stopped and literally took his hand in mine (yep I'm really sentimental) and said, "Can I just tell you how thankful we are to work with you. I have heard so many horrible stories from different filmmakers that got really messed over by their sales reps, and I feel the complete opposite, I love working with you and feel blessed everyday by our relationship." His response was, "We feel the same way about you guys. Do you know how many sales reps complain about the producers of their movies being difficult to work with? When we sign a movie, we really sign people. That's why we only pick a select few and its most important that we like the people."

I could go on and on with so many more stories of how kindness spreads like wild fire and brings beautiful outcomes to those involved.

I have witnessed some really horrific treatment of people on film sets. I have yet to understand why or how the people involved think this behavior will benefit their film or their future. In all aspects of life: how we treat people will always come back around. Whether you're the boss or the person who retrieves the coffee, kindness will get you were money never can and a rotten attitude will halt you in your tracks.

This business is completely built upon relationships; PROTECT them with all your might!

It's a small town . . . Always Be Kind!

13. Find a "Tribe" Outside of the Film Industry

I joined Instagram because my fitness trainer of eight years Tracy Anderson was holding a contest through that platform. I honestly didn't join because I wanted to have millions of followers, or even to promote my films; I just wanted to win a competition. Little did I know that small decision in my life would have the most rewarding beautiful outcome I could ever image! I became a member of the #tamily, which is a community of women all across the world who connect and share their passion for Tracy's method.

I don't know about you but sometimes I get so wrapped up in the film industry it's hard to see outside of Hollywood. Most of my friends work in the biz, and I often find myself engrossed in conversations that are solely centered on making movies. While there is nothing wrong with that, and I thrive off my relationships in my industry, I also feel allot of the time I have nothing else to talk about.

Joining the #tamily, has given me a community outside of my everyday world, and I cherish these women more than words could express. Most of them I have never met face to face, but they inspire, encourage, and love on me every day. It's a gorgeous life giving community that lifts one another up, listens when someone is down and cheers when a milestone has been reached. This group is a wonderful example of how social media can change people's lives for the better.

I encourage other filmmakers to join a community completely apart from their profession. It actually makes me a better storyteller when I am connecting everyday with women in the world. This is so important for me as a female driven moviemaker. Hollywood can feel like a little bubble, and it's important to break out of it every once in awhile.

I joined a soccer league recently and was excited to be a part of a team. But since my team is located here in Los Angeles most of the members work in the film industry, therefore I found myself the other day, yet again gabbing away on the bench about making movies and the rise and fall of the DVD industry.

The ladies from #tamily also support me in a way that is very hard for people who work in show business to do. Because none of them are trying to "make it" in the business, their words of encouragement and love towards the things I am creating really gives me the confidence I need to continue to conquer a very challenging career path. I feel truly lifted up by them, because deep down they are not in competition with me. Jealousy is a part of human nature, and sometimes I think it can be a challenge to not compare to someone else. And this is why I believe in the importance of finding people to commune with that have nothing to do with "making it" in Hollywood.

This is where social media has had an incredible impact on the world. You can connect with the push of a button to someone living in on the other side of the planet.

My #tamily members encourage me to be healthy and stay fit, nothing wrong with a little of that in your life.

I am a HUGE advocate for finding your filmmaking tribe, I love mine, but I also encourage you to find a tribe that flourishes you in another aspect of your life. It just might be the life changing "team" you never knew you needed.

14. Is Your Agent Sabotaging Your Career?

As an actress turned producer my eyes have really been opened to the negative effect agents can have on their actors' careers. The scary thing is that the actor probably has no idea what is going on.

I produce indie films. My films have sold to large distribution companies and have gone on to sell on the shelves of Wal-Mart and Hastings, available on Amazon, iTunes and Netflix.

Our budgets are still micro, but we are building an audience and growing bigger each time. So you can imagine my shock when we go to hire a local actor (with maybe a couple of IMDB credits) and their agent comes back with a list of demands that only a name actor that pulls in a large audience could ask for.

On one of our feature films we cast many roles locally. We really liked two of the actors we auditioned for the lead role in the film and it was a knife's edge as to whom we would pick.

After a lot of debate we made our decision. I called this particular actor to offer the SAG New Media paid leading role in our film and was a little surprised by his attitude on the phone. He was not excited and had more questions than I expected of a kid who was "getting a break". We called another actor to offer him a different role in the movie and his enthusiasm, excitement, and kind spirit was contagious.

A day later I got a call from the agent of the actor to whom we had offered the "lead" role. She went on to make crazy demands for her client like points in the back end (beyond SAG residuals), a trailer on set, per diem, five star accommodations . . . and she insulted my film in the process. I kept telling her, "your client has never made a movie, why would we give him all of these things?"

Listen people, when you hold no cards you can't have a full house.

I was shocked she wasn't ecstatic that her client was offered the lead role in a movie opposite a star name. I got off the phone thinking, 'I don't want to cast this kid anymore, because I know his agent is going to be difficult to work with. Set is full of enough stress; I don't want to add any more troubles to my production.

We immediately retracted our offer to that actor and I called up the other actor to give him the good news. He was now the lead in the movie. He was excited, grateful, generous, and a blast to work with.

Want to know the fate of these two actors? Garrett Westton, who graciously accepted the lead role in the film, was portrayed on the cover of our DVD that graces the shelves of Wal-Mart today.

He moved to Los Angeles, landed an agent and was recently seen in the Disney show, "Best Friends Whenever." His performance in the film is viewable in five countries and counting. I have no doubt he has a bright and beautiful future ahead of him, not only because he is insanely talented and good-looking, but also because he is smart, kind, and easy to work with.

The actor who was too good for our little movie, and whose agent insulted our film, was most recently seen by one of our crew members, doing extra work in his hometown area.

I really want to shine a light on this issue and share what I have learned. Maybe it will save an actor out there from losing a part they really wanted, a role that could change their career and ultimately, their life.

You might not be aware of what your agent is doing behind your back. I had this experience this experience on my film "Wish For Christmas." Thank goodness we really liked the person and worked it out with them, because we were on the verge of moving on to a different actor without a second glance. **Don't forget there are hundreds of people right behind you.**

If your agent seems difficult, I assume the actor might be too, and unless you are Brad Pitt or a star name that is going to sell your movie at the marketplace, a producer just doesn't have the energy or time to deal with insane demands or unnecessary egos.

Did I mention we take direct submissions for our movies? These actors have submitted themselves, come in for the audition on their own, and then once cast, the agent materializes and begins to negotiate on the actor's behalf. Most actors don't know that these emails are even being sent or what they say.

If you submit yourself for a project and you've worked things out with the producers, do not allow your agent to get in there and start sabotaging a deal that you already put into place. It's very frustrating for the producers and frankly a big waste of time.

My advice is to stay in close communication with your agent and the producer, so you are one hundred percent aware of what's going on. Be wise enough to know when you need your agent to get involved and when you don't. If you have been cast in a low budget indie movie, there is no room to negotiate, because low budget films have very little money and there are fifty people lined up behind you wanting that part.

Remember, the world owes you nothing, be grateful, don't be a problem!

15. Small Town Hollywood

It is completely against the grain of Hollywood to go to a small town to make a movie. Especially when that town doesn't have a strong film community or film incentives. But one of the many highlights of shooting "Catching Faith" was working with a very small community in the Chippewa Valley area of Wisconsin. We broke the rules in this area, and we succeeded because we had faith in ourselves and the people we surrounded ourselves with.

Crazy to think only a few months ago I was sifting through resumes and headshots lining up the soon to be cast and crew for "The Elijah Project." Most of the resumes were from people who had never set foot on a movie set a day in their life, and to be honest, I was a nervous wreck leading up to day one on set. Half of our crew had never done film work before, and most of our cast was beginners. We handpicked people based on their willingness to learn, and their enthusiasm for the project.

Our instincts proved right when day one rolled around and everything ran as smoothly as an average Hollywood movie set. Our new team jumped into their positions with gusto and confidence, excelling beyond our expectations, using their applicable skills to perform a job they had never done.

We traveled in most of the heads of each department from out of state, and it was exciting to watch them lead the way, teaching skills to people who would never normally get the opportunity to work on a large movie set.

In the beginning of developing this project we looked at many states that had film incentives, Massachusetts, New Mexico and Louisiana, to name a few. But after my filmmaking partner and I had spent the winter in Chippewa Falls writing the script with my sister, who happens to live in the town, word got out about the movie. So many people reached out to us, asking how they could help, that we chose the Chippewa Valley for the location for our movie. A huge element of our movie was football, and since we had such a small budget to work with, when the local semi pro teams agreed to be in our film, that really got the ball rolling. We met with locals about using their houses in the film, along with a private Catholic High school, and that sealed the deal. We made the decision to shoot the film in Eau Claire and Chippewa Falls, and the in kind favors we received out weighed the film incentive's other states offered.

Every day we put up notices on Facebook to the community for things we needed (also an amazing tool for indie filmmakers), and it created a beautiful bridge between a film crew and a community excited to be involved. It gave people the ability to be included and to our amazement, requests were granted with open arms. One day while shooting at the local high school football field, we were in desperate need of a gator for a tracking shot. The one we had secured with the school broke down before we arrived, and immediately we started making phone calls to local's and put an ad out on our Facebook page. Within hours a man showed up with a tow track, he unlatched the back of the truck to reveal a gator, and said, "I heard you needed this."

This is just one of the many stories of how this community came through for our movie.

This experience has given me a new outlook on bringing a film to a rural area. Not only because the town was excited to help, instead of finding ways to hinder the production, but also because throughout this journey friendships were developed in the most unexpected ways, passions were discovered, and talents created.

A film set uses so many different people's abilities, utilizing the skills of such diverse talents as a writer, forklift operator, hairdresser, and even someone who can brew a good cup of coffee. There is an adage that "it takes a village to raise a child", the same can be said for making a film. That is why it makes sense to partner with a community, and pull from the talents in that town.

It was exciting to witness people who never in a million years would have thought to go after work in the film biz, discover a passion they never knew they had.

When searching for the head of the hair and makeup department, it only made sense to hire a woman who owned her own salon. Even though she had never done hair and makeup for the screen, she had years of experience doing this job for a living. The director sent her some websites on how to create looks for film, and with just a few days of research she was ready to perform on our set. An opportunity that she would have never gotten had we not decided to shoot in her town. The head of our Art Department was also a local hire, and she used the skills she learned from serving in the US Army to survive the rigorous hours on a movie set, and nothing got past her insane attention to detail.

Many of our first time crew members had a lot of theater experience, and everyone utilized the Internet to learn how to conquer a film position for the first time. Everyone has to start somewhere, and bringing this movie to a small town gave opportunity and experience to locals eager for the chance to work on a film set. I am extremely proud as a producer to have nurtured people and encouraged them. They could do their job without fear, because we were all in this together. Believing in and encouraging people is the first step to building a team that will be self sufficient and confident in their abilities.

I went from being afraid of the unknown to being grateful we produced "Catching Faith" in the most unlikely place. I couldn't have asked for a better group of people, and a more embracing community that surrounded our movie with love and generosity. It truly was a special experience for everyone. In turn, our film looks amazing, all because of the kindness and talents of this small community.

I am a big believer in breaking the rules in the Hollywood handbook. I love when people tell me something isn't possible, or that it's a bad idea, because then our team turns around and proves them wrong. Don't be afraid to go outside of the box! Find a unique way of accomplishing your dream project. Fear holds us all back, everything is possible, and when you remove fear from your mind, you can reach far beyond your imagination. Don't be afraid! Reach out to the community around you; you never know what gems may be hiding just out of your sight.

16. It Only Gets Bigger, Not Better

"It only gets bigger not better." My acting coach Harry Mastrogeorge used to say this all of the time pertaining to success. He would warn his students that all the issues you have, whatever they may be while you're struggling, wouldn't get better when you succeeded. They would only get bigger.

While making our first feature film, we felt stressed out, but it was NOTHING compared to the stress of our second movie. Because you see our first film was only our own money, and if we lost it, no big deal. But with our second movie, we had the pressure of other people's money and the eyes of more people upon us. Failure was not an option. Not that it ever is, but the stress was bigger, not better, as we became more successful in this business.

They say your sophomore film is harder than your freshman. I think it is expectations, and the pressure you feel as more people depend on you to deliver the goods on time, in good quality.

I wrote a whole article on "being ready to take outside investment" and I feel even stronger now that I have completed a film with other people's money. It is a HUGE responsibility that we did not take lightly, and every day on set, as we ran the show, I never forgot for a moment that I had to deliver this to someone who had given us their hard earned money, relying we would not let them down.

Be prepared as your star rises, with great things comes great responsibility. So wherever you are in life, it's best to work on your issues now, because success doesn't solve your problems, in fact it can end up being a big magnifying glass for them.

So get healthy, be prepared, and don't ever say, "When this happens…I'll be happy," cause you just might spend the rest of your life waiting in purgatory. Be content with where you are, enjoy the journey, and only accept outside money when you know without a shadow of a doubt you can deliver a finished product.

FILMMAKING

17. Imagination Is More Important Than Knowledge

"Imagination is more important than Knowledge." – Albert Einstein

I first heard this quote by Albert Einstein in my acting class with Harry. He would use this as an example to an actor, who had never had the life experience of the character they were playing. But he encouraged us to imagine ourselves in those circumstances and promised us that with time it would become real to us through our imagination. This is a key element, in my opinion, in the actor's journey. My practice of sitting down alone and imagining myself in the life experiences of the character were life changing as an actor. Every word I spoke as the character became real to me. What originally was impossible with my knowledge became possible through my imagination.

This philosophy has rolled over into my life as an entrepreneur and artist. This is what we get to do, to live in a world of daydreaming, in our creations; we get to get down and dirty and play in it. What a fun job! Harry always used children as an example of the mindset you must have to be a full and rich actor. You must believe with all your might that what you are doing is so real no one can tell you differently. Watch children play and see how engrossed they are in their world, and with such conviction they believe it without a shadow of a doubt. Harry would always say, "Get in your sandbox and start kicking up sand."

Being back in the home I grew up in, I found myself out in the woods behind my parents' house. Trudging up the wooded hills I was transported to my little self, running around these trees. Playing make believe and creating stories in my head. Those woods were everything from the medieval times to the wild wild west. They were the streets of New York to the countryside of France. I was reminded of why I wanted to get into this business in the first place. I wanted to tell stories and recreate my imagination. I wish I still had the fantasies of my eight-year-old self, never questioning my instincts, completely engrossed in my world, no one could tell me differently. As we grow up, we lose so much of our childhood innocence. We begin to doubt ourselves and question everything. Maybe even to a fault. We have an idea, and then doubt and fear creep in rearing their ugly heads, and we give up before we even begin.

As we get older and life disappoints us or we disappoint our lives, it's easy to become bitter, angry, and fearful. All of these things squelch the creative spirit and make it impossible to soar through the depths to the height of our imagination. Which is like free falling with no fear of hitting the ground, because there is no ground. Imagination is bottomless.

Einstein also said, "Knowledge is limited, imagination encircles the world."

Those are some powerful words. As artists we can't be limited; we must scour the deepest parts of our creativity to discover what does not exist. Imagination is to make the invisible-visible.

Everything begins with an idea. The true test is having the courage to take that idea and wrestle with it until it is a reality. I love the visual of wrestling, because you are going to get dirty and frustrated and you are going to scream a lot! But you cannot let your opponent-fear of failure-win. You must endure through the pain of the perils to come out on the other side and hold up your trophy of triumph.

The other day I was on set working as a stand-in and as I was waiting in the holding area I was going over some video numbers for our app game. I had found a glitch in the game and was writing down our code to send to our programmer. A gentleman sitting next to me asked me what I was doing. After I explained to him I was part of a team that had created an app game, he asked me, "Where did you get that numbering system?" I replied, "We created it; we made it up."

There was no blue print for the kind of game we wanted to make, so we invented our own blue print. If an outsider was to look at the inner details of our game it would look like a convoluted mess, but we as the inventors understand it all. What an extraordinary gift we have: one of the five inward senses is imagination. We as human beings are so blessed to embody it, and I wonder how much we really utilize it?

I have been inspired by so many people in my life, especially my brother Alex Boylan. In 2006 we were living together in Los Angeles, and I remember this story like it was yesterday. I was sitting in the living room of our apartment when he came bursting out of his room beaming with enthusiasm. "I have an idea," he stated, and then went on to explain to me how he wanted to create a fully online interactive reality show called "Around the World For Free" where the host had to get around the world with no money, completely relying on the kindness of strangers. The audience would tell him where to go, and who to stay with, and he would go. After finishing his thoughts he said, "I'm going to go make this happen." He went back in his room, shut the door, and began figuring out how to make this idea of the first interactive on line reality show a reality. In 2007 he launched the series on the CBS Morning Show, and it has now had three successful season. He was tenacious and I watched as he battled this completely unknown terrain, overcoming extreme challenges, never giving up or wavering in his pursuit. He has never stopped being an inspiration to me. I look at him with awe, and think if he can do it, I can do it. There was a time in my life when I was envious of him.

Realizing what a waste of time this was, I began to learn from him and allow his journey to inspire and encourage mine.

I live by the philosophy that the answer is already "no" if I don't ask, and I have already "failed" if I never try. So I have nothing to lose because I had nothing to begin with. I wake up in the morning reminding myself to live with this fearless attitude, which gives me unseen strength to go after the things that could be deemed impossible. If I have an idea, and if I use my imagination, I can make the invisible, visible with the courage and tenacity to press through to the finish line.

Where would we be if the greatest minds in history never explored their "what if" ideas?

Do you have an idea you are dying to create? Why not start taking the steps TODAY to make it a reality TOMORROW. Have you been imagining something for a while, but don't think you have the knowledge to pull it off? Start experimenting NOW with ways to take nothing and turn it into something. The world may be a better place if YOU take that first step today!

Believe that anything is possible!

18. Let's Talk "in Real Time"

After years of making content, i.e.: web series, shorts, a play, a feature film, and even now an app game, I have learned the lesson of how much time everything takes.

I am a person who wants everything yesterday, and patience has never been my strong suit. Every time I begin a project, I think, "O this will only take a few months," and of course a year and a half later, the project is still in the making.

I wanted to write about this because I think it is so important for people to be aware of the time things take, and to not get discouraged when things don't happen fast. I feel like since I struggle with this, I'm sure there must be others out there that struggle with it as well.

The key to success is following through, and staying the course, even when the road gets bumpy. Since nothing happens overnight, it is so important to be passionate about the project you are embarking on. That is what will keep you motivated when obstacles begin to fly your way.

The greatest example I can share is my latest endeavor, a live action app game for the iPhone. My team and I began the process in January of last year. We all met in my living room, and set out to use our filmmaking skills to incorporate into a game. We estimated the process would only take a few months, and the game would be released by the summer of 2012. BOY, were we wrong, but thankfully everyone involved was incredibly dedicated and never gave up. We began writing in January of 2012, and our plan was to spend a month shooting. We shot for five days a week, eight to ten hour days, and it took four months to complete principle photography. Then we moved into the editing process, which took AGAIN longer than we had expected. The game finally made it in the programmer's hands, and is available today.

I want to encourage people to follow through in whatever path they are on. When I was younger I would give up so easily thinking, "This is impossible". I would almost give up before I even started. But commitment is a habit, we can learn and nurture in time. And I have found that once I have completed a project I am addicted, and I can't wait to do it all over again.

No human is an island, and you must surround yourself with like minded people, dedicated, talented hardworking folks, who will follow through until the end.

Just go out there and do it! If you don't do it, you automatically fail. So really there is nothing to lose. There is no better time than TODAY to begin!

19. My Year Living Out of a Suitcase…and Still Going Strong

A few months ago I was walking out of an event, and in my bubbling, little, happy-go-lucky self I handed my valet ticket to the man behind the counter and smiled, "How are you tonight?"

Feeling all confident, excited, and inspired by what I had just learned after hours listening to experts in the filmmaking field, I was not expecting the response on the other end.

"Horrible, I hate this job," he grumbled as he grabbed my ticket.

I was taken aback, and then said in my most supportive voice, "Well then why are you working here?"

His face grew dark and he raised his voice at me, saying, "Because nobody will give me my big break, I'm a singer, and no one will give me a shot, no one will give it to me."

I stood there for a moment taking in his energy and I responded with my gentle understanding of years of experience doing a job I hate-waiting for someone to knock on my door and say, "Oh, there you are, I have been looking everywhere for you!"-And said, "And no one ever will. You need to choose yourself and give yourself the opportunities in life that you want. It is no one's fault that you are where you are. You are the only one responsible for your future."

His face grew gentle and he said, "Wow I never thought about it like that."

As my car pulled up, I said, "Go out there and change your life. Choose yourself and create work for yourself."

He smiled and said, "I will."

And I got in my car and drove off.

I really hope that man is changing his mentality, and his actions. Because I have learned, no one is GOING TO GIVE IT TO YOU! That's just not the way life works. Well maybe if you are born with a silver spoon dangling out of your mouth, and then maybe life would be too easy and you wouldn't even try.

The whole drive home I contemplated over this conversation. I even probably forgot everything I learned at the event, as I couldn't get this man's words out of my head. Everything he said was, "no one will give me, me, me!" And

I grew frustrated at this mentality, and angry with this guy, only to realize I wasn't mad at him. He had put a mirror up to myself and how I used to live my life in this place of frustration. And this conversation brought up all those yucky feelings, washing over me. And yes I had given up the frustrating beggar artist life, traded it for the extremely challenging entrepreneur life. But I realized as I drove home that I had forgotten to tell him "neither path in life is the easy path."

At this point in my life I had been living out of a suitcase for eight months in order to make my second feature film a reality. I was exhausted as my husband and I traveled around the country living in other people's spaces, trying to create our future film.

So let me rewind to the beginning of this journey and explain how I became a vagabond traveling homeless filmmaker!

Late August of 2013, I packed a suitcase, boarded a plane and never returned to my apartment, and I never will.

That year after accepting a crew position on an HBO miniseries I packed one suitcase and headed to my childhood hometown in Massachusetts. A month into my job my husband/film partner called me and said, "I think we need to give up our apartment and move to your sister's house in Chippewa Falls, Wisconsin and get this script written and completed."

Well as you can imagine, my jaw hit the floor, and I began to have heart palpitations. "But I'm not even there to pack up the place!" I pleaded, as I looked at my one suitcase that was supposed to last me three months, thinking now must last me…as long as need be.

"Don't worry I'll take care of everything, and get our cars dealt with too."

His generosity to do everything made me feel guilty as my blood boiled inside, thinking about how I wouldn't have closure with our beautiful gorgeous apartment and "life" in Hancock Park, California. I would never see it again, and for some reason I was shaking and unable to hold back tears. "Do you want to make a movie or not?" he asked sternly.

"Yes" my voice quivered back.

"Then we have to give it up!" he replied. Now let me just add here, we didn't have money in the bank to shoot this movie, and everything was still in conception at the time, but truth was that after spending months trying to write a script in Google docs from different states with my sister, we realized it was becoming an impossible task. I nodded my headed, he was right, it was time to make a sacrifice to try and secure a possible future in filmmaking.

When my show ended in late November I boarded a plane and flew to my new home in Wisconsin, dealing with the sadness of ending a show, the loss of my beloved apartment, and the bitter cold of winter I fell into a depression and I struggled to wake up every morning to write the script with my partners. I have seasonal depression, and it happened to be the coldest winter in the area, in one hundred years. I struggled with keeping my positive attitude every single day. Most days were negative 30 degrees below and we couldn't even go outside. I felt like a prisoner and my soul was being crushed as I thrive off my afternoon walks in sunny California. My husband continued to encourage me as I struggled with the unknown, the risk we were taking with no guarantee. His optimistic attitude kept me going, and I am so grateful for such an amazing partner. There were days when I didn't even want to be in my own skin, I hated myself, and I thought I was spiraling into a hole I would never crawl out of. I love my sister and her family, but as someone who thrives off being busy, it was hard to write for four hours a day, and then sit in a house waiting for time to go by. I longed to return home, and be active in my social community. Honestly those three months were a very low time for me, and without seeing the end of the tunnel I began to lose hope. I kept thinking, "This movie better happen, we better get the money, this better pay off."

And when January rolled around and the script was in a good place I pleaded with my husband to head back west. After acquiring so many locations, and help from the community of the Chippewa Valley, we were certain we would shoot the movie there in June of that year, but I couldn't spend another day in the gloomy cold weather. I was worried my depression wouldn't lift, and I didn't even know who I was anymore. I had to find sunlight, and I had to find it fast.

John and I packed up my car, and left in the end of January, driving twenty-three hours straight from Wisconsin to New Mexico.

The next day it was 70 degrees in New Mexico and as I dragged my dog on a three-hour walk, I felt the sadness lift and my spirits rise. I learned seasonal depression is a REAL thing, and I REALLY have it. I now know my limits. I can't be in cold weather for long periods of time, but BOY am I thankful we did it.

BECAUSE in the end we DID complete production on "Catching Faith."

Fast forward to today, in hindsight, the courage and determination that we put into creating this project was "Worth It." Everything we sacrificed, led to one of my most incredible life experiences to date, that I will cherish forever. I'm so glad I am not bitter and angry, waiting for someone to GIVE it to me; I grasped the opportunity and ran with it.

And all the things that seemed so important to me, our apartment (a few walls, a room and a kitchen), all my belongings trapped in storage (can't even remember what's in there) and a place to call my own (I never owned it anyway), are NOT even close to my most precious possession NOW, the shiny silver hard drive sitting on the counter. Inside it holds my hopes, dreams, and FUTURE.

And believe me this life as an artist is HARD, but remember if it were easy everyone would be doing it!

20. Turn Opportunity into Your Passion Project

If you had told me five years ago I was going to be making "faith-based films" I would have laughed out loud. Not that I had any problem with them, just that I was not even close to being on that kind of filmmaking path.

My first feature film was a horror/thriller, and my follow-up script to that was a supernatural thriller about a girl who works overnight shifts in a haunted nursing home. I was in the process of trying to get that movie financed when the opportunity to make a faith based family football movie was presented to me. I immediately went home and started writing a faith based family film. **When a door opens, walk through it immediately. No, don't walk. Run!**

I think people were surprised to find out I was going to make this kind of film, not because I wasn't a Christian, because I am, but because "faith-based" films tend to be cheesy and sub-par. I decided I would change that. I am going to make quality "faith based" films for this generation. It was an exciting endeavor, and I wasn't afraid of what people thought of me. I am going to change how people view the genre.

I immediately started watching faith-based films to get a feel for this genre. I was extremely disappointed to witness the representation of women. They are often trying to hold the man back in some way, either their faith or their life, and in turn giving the man the appearance of being more "holy" or "better" than the woman. I also noticed it is often the men bringing people in the film to faith, teaching important lessons, and being the lead character. I decided this was my opportunity to be the change I want to see in the world.

We were given some guidelines for the film, which included football. So we found a way to tell a story from the female point of view while also focusing a big chunk of the movie on football. Instead of the typical story of a male driven football movie, we thought outside the box, and told a very relevant story from the female protagonist's point of view.

When an opportunity comes your way, MAKE it be whatever you want it to be!

When my film "Catching Faith" released, the excitement from women who appreciated seeing themselves represented positively on screen was overwhelming.

I spent many years holding on very tightly to my "plan" and that forcefulness didn't get me very far. I have learned that the more open we are to the opportunities that come our way, the greater chance we have of reaching the success we want.

I have yet to get that supernatural thriller off the ground, but I have now finished two faith-based family films, and am currently writing the next one. Imagine if I turned down that opportunity and waited to try to get my other script made. I'd probably still be waiting, and would have missed out on the incredible life experiences that have come from being a part of bringing my last two films to life.

You never know what possibilities lie ahead, and if you're holding on too tightly to "one" dream, you might be missing out on the other "one".

21. Five Tips for First Time Independent Filmmakers

1. Find your tribe.

The most important element of making an indie film is the team behind the project. Everyone is building their team for the future, so either find a team you want to collaborate and rise with, or find people to build your team. We have our core group that we will work with forever, as long as they continue to want to work with us. We are not just a filmmaking team; we are a family. And take care of your crew, first rule of indie filmmaking, treat everyone with respect and kindness. Trust me, it goes a long, long way!

2. Write a screenplay around what you have, they say write what you know, well I say write what locations you have access to.

My entire feature was written completely around the house and surrounding areas that were offered to us to make a movie in. My husband and I went out to the location and took pictures of every nook and cranny; we then brought the pictures back to our screenplay writer, and he wrote scenes according to what we had. Location is one of the biggest hurdles when shooting a film, so find a great place that you have access to, and then write a story around it.

3. Make a film that is sellable.

You might have a passion project that matters to you, but this industry is a business and highly competitive, and there is a good chance no one cares about your passion project. Investors want to make money, distribution companies want to make money, and sales reps want to make money. See a pattern here? Yep! Everyone wants to make money, so if your film isn't marketable there is a good chance no one will give you money to make it, and no one will buy it to distribute it. Find out what is selling in the marketplace before jumping into making a film.

4. For your first feature film, make it for a small budget.

Don't put yourself in a position where you won't be able to re-coup your investment. The marketplace is changing, and distribution companies are not paying much up front for films these days, if they even pay anything up front at all. Make your first feature for as cheap as possible and, honestly be willing to lose the money. You might never see that money again, so don't spend anything you're not willing to lose.

5. Cast actors who you know will be supportive on and off the set.

When making an indie film, everyone needs to be helpful on set because chances are you will have very few crewmembers, and will need every helping hand possible. Have an open dialogue with your actors before casting them, so they understand the expectations, and want to be a part of the whole process of filming. Also, cast actors who have strong social media presence, and people they know will help promote the film when it releases. TRUST ME, you will need all the help you can get when the time comes to market your film, and it is extremely important that your whole team is spreading the word, and sharing the news.

I hope these five tips where helpful to you, as you embark on your awesome adventure into the world of independent filmmaking. Good luck, and just do it!

22. Hire a Woman!

This year I won the lottery!

The Screen Actors Guild awards lottery that is I was chosen to sit on the SAG nominating committee! I was overjoyed as you can imagine, because this is like winning the Hollywood jackpot. Imagine if every movie from this past year started flooding into your mailbox.

The ballot came the other day and I tore open the envelope like a little kid tearing open a first Christmas present, excitement filling my body, as I was ready to make my choices for the all the Best Actors. I opened the pages and was completely taken aback to find a significant difference in the number of choices I had for males vs. females. The list of male actors I had to choose from for Best Actor filled an entire page, whereas the female list was only about a quarter of a page. I felt my blood begin to boil under my skin, sitting in complete confusion and frustration as to why I wasn't given an equal number of options for each category.

So I decided to do a little research and I found this startling statistic.

"Female characters accounted for only 15% of protagonists in the 100 highest-grossing domestic films of 2013, according to the study "It's a Man's (Celluloid) World" by veteran researcher Martha Lauzen, executive director of the Center for the Study of Women in Television and Film at San Diego State University."

Why are there still so few women in front of and behind the camera in the year 2017. I have been hoping that if we had more females in power positions then that would translate into more strong female characters in front of the camera and more women working behind it. Sadly, the answer is still probably, "No."

I recently attended a Women In Film event where I had the pleasure of hearing a very established female producer speak.

She shared an astonishing story with us that still haunts me.

She told us she was at an event sitting next to a woman who ran a major studio. The studio executive was telling her how they were looking for directors for a particular show and she had put the word out and received a list with ten names on it. Our speaker had asked her how many female directors were on the list. The woman looked at her for a moment and then answered in a quiet voice, "None."

Our speaker said she scolded that woman for not standing up for her fellow females. The woman actually said she hadn't even thought about the fact that not a single woman made the list. SHAME on her and shame on all the women who don't hire and support females in this industry.

This woman is in an incredible position to hire females, where normally a man would get hired. When a woman has that opportunity she needs to grasp it for the sake of us all.

Women, who have achieved powerful positions, must hire and go to bat for each other. We must think in terms of rising together.

While in pre-production on my feature film "Catching Faith," I received a slew of resumes for each department. If I had a resume from a man and a woman with equal qualifications, I hired the woman. We had a female electrician, a female first assistant director, a female art director, and the list goes on. As a female producer it was very important to me to hire as many women as possible, and to give jobs to the ladies, where normally a man would be the first choice.

There is too much competitiveness within the female community, and the reason may be because there are so few jobs for women. We must be the change we want to see. It must start somewhere, with someone, and we can each chisel away bit by bit. If we spend more time and energy fighting for each other, instead of clamoring over each other, we may be able to shift the paradigm. If we re-adjust our thinking we can shape the future.

Men are more than happy to work and collaborate with the opposite sex, but honestly for the most part I think men just don't think to hire a female in a crew position on a movie set. It is not that they don't want to work with us; it is that it is not the norm for them to think of us for a job. Chances are a man would hire a man before a woman. I even made this a survey on a set I am currently working on, and all of the men answered my question with "I would hire a man for that job." It is not the norm to hire a female grip or electrician, so it is up to us to make it the norm.

This is all a work in progress and we can't wait for someone else to do it.

It starts with you and me!

When there isn't plenty of room at the top, we need to create the room.

So the next time you sit down to write a script, think about changing the hero to the heroine. When you're in pre-production on a film, give your fellow female resumes a second glance. The next time you are in post production, hire a female editor.

Let's be the change we want to see in the film industry today.

23. Solidarity

Maybe it's my Libra side, everything must be fair and equal, but I really love to watch a project unfold with the creative perspective of both sexes.

Last week I attended the BANFF Convention, where I was very disappointed to sit and listen to panel after panel of men sharing their work and opinions about what is next in the entertainment industry.

There was even a representative there for Up.tv which is a woman-driven channel, and guess what? A man was representing it. I grew frustrated and fidgety in my seat, looking around a room filled with more woman than men and had to ask myself, "What the heck! Why can't they can't bring in some ladies to speak?"

Now, I'm not saying I want to replace all the men with women, but I do want us to have a seat at the table. I want to hear a woman's perspective as well as a man's. And hey, I'm sure the men in the audience would have liked to hear a woman up there talking as well!

I had the pleasure of working on a film with Helenna Santos, and Barry Morgan. They were producing partners on their project, The Infected, and I enjoyed watching their fantastic dynamic together. The film has an equal cast of women and men. Helenna and Barry collaborated on the story, and guess what? The lead female isn't just a stupid girl who runs around naked and oblivious to what's going on around her, which can sometimes be the trend in horror flicks. Thank you Barry and Helenna. It was refreshing as a female actor to work with both a woman and a man calling the shots!

I had the same experience acting in a feature film called, "Rabid Love" where Hayley Derryberry and her husband Paul Porter, collaborated with such ease. I felt so comfortable with them, and I loved having a female producer who understood my needs as a woman on set. Many years ago I was working on a horror film as an actress when the director and producer started disagreeing over the scene (both men) they took their discussion out of the room and left me strapped to a chair freezing cold, covered in blood and completely uncomfortable for over thirty minutes. Fast forward to me working with Hayley and Paul, where I, as an actress, again had to get covered in blood and lay on the freezing cold ground. The difference this time was that Paul and Hayley were extremely concerned for me and the other actress. Hayley and Paul worked fast to get the shots we needed and get us out of the cold ASAP.

What Barry and Paul have in common is that they are excited and ready to make smart female driven films. They know that women have equally good ideas as men. They aren't threatened working along-side a woman to get the job done right!

I am the only female producer on our next feature film, along with four men. Our story centers on a female character and if my voice wasn't heard, I could only imagine how distorted our story would become. I have seen so many female-driven films, and I can always tell when it was only men in the writing room. I'm not saying it can't be done, but for the most part it is glaringly obvious when there is no female voice in the collaboration. Men can definitely write a woman's story, just like a woman can write a man's story, but that, is the exception to the rule.

In order to tell stories for all different types of people, we need all different types of people in the creative room. Women and men alike! And entertainment needs to stop fearing female lead movies. They make money, a lot of money! And it's time for the female voice to step in and take a place at the table; writing, producing, editing and directing!

And to finish up, I must quote Cate Blanchet, who said once at the academy awards, *"And thank you to… those of us in the industry who are still foolishly clinging to the idea that female films, with a woman at the center, are niche audiences. They are not—audiences want to see them and, in fact, they earn money. The world is round, people."*

Amen Sister!

I think we are on to something here with the idea of a woman and man teaming up to bring a project to life. As a female filmmaker, my smartest choices are surrounding myself with incredibly open-minded men and women. The people who listen to me, and respect what I have to say, and vice versa.

We have the power to choose who we work with. Its up to us to find amazing people to partner with, because it is not girls VS. boys, it is all of US working together to create the best story that touches every person in the audience.

24. How to make a TRUE Guerilla Indie Film

In honor of my feature film "Home Sweet Home" releasing in the U.S. from Image Entertainment, I thought it would be appropriate to share our experience making a movie in true indie style.

First I must give a huge shout out to the team that made this movie. I always say, "You don't need a lot of people, you just need the right people."

"Home Sweet Home" is the perfect example of this.

After my husband and business partner John KD Graham and I had finished making a web series and a bunch of short films together, we thought it was time to take the plunge and make a feature film. The process seemed daunting as we had never tackled such a huge endeavor, but little by little we pieced together the puzzle, and never gave up, with an outcome being a fantastic indie thriller. Each day we tackled something new, and the key to our success was never looking too far into the future, or we would have been so overwhelmed, we would have given up on day one! We just took it one day at a time, which is really all you can do anyway.

Our first question was what did we want the story to be. This led us to SETTING-where could we film the movie with no budget to actually pay for a location. So once we had the location we then wrote a script around that property. We had asked John KD Graham's parents if we could shoot the movie at their house, which lies on eighteen acres of land out in La Luz, NM. They agreed, and we worked with our screenwriter, my brother Andrew Boylan, using all the nooks and crannies of the property to weave into the story line. The house already had some fantastic features that added high production design to the film without having to spend a penny. We utilized the entire property, and again went against the grain of a horror movie, and instead of being in the woods, we trap the victim in the desert with nowhere to run or hide. Aware of the fact we were working with no real budget, we decided to film the majority of the movie in broad daylight. The location is pitch dark when the sun goes down, and we knew we couldn't afford the lights it would take to shoot night scenes. But in the end it was another awesome aspect of taking a genre and flipping it on its head.

This became the best decision we could have ever made, to successfully attempt such a huge endeavor. John and I were driving to Arizona to shoot a video for a ranch when we brainstormed many different thriller ideas that could all take place in one house. With all the news articles about squatters, we got excited about making a home invasion film-in reverse. "What if you came home to your house, to discover you were the invader?"

Researching how to raise money for a low budget film led us to Kickstarter, where we set up an account and asked friends and family to contribute to our film. John and I spent days online reaching out to everyone we knew asking them to help us make this movie, and in turn we offered rewards to the backers. Our campaign was a success and we moved forward with the finances we had raised. In fact, our kickstarter page is still there if you would like to view what we put together for our campaign.

Next we went into pre-production, securing actors who were dear friends and willing to come to the middle of nowhere to shoot an indie. John and I didn't have any money to offer people, but one thing we promised was that we would complete the movie, no matter what, even if it was just to show our friends and family. We offered travel, food, and beds/sleeping bags, and the amazing cast and crew came on board, all for the sheer love of the making movies.

Since we all lived on location while filming, literally sleeping on the floor or in trailers next to each other, we had to have a group of people that could all get along well.

Our crew had all been working together for years. They all come from working on big budget New Mexico films like "Thor, Avengers," "True Grit," "Cowboys and Aliens," so we had the best of the best! Our team had already made many short films together, so the flow and ease of shooting was effortless. John's mother cooked meals for us, and would do runs into town for props we needed.

The group pitched in with equipment, and all the locations we found were donated to us from the community, including a convenience store that allowed us to shoot a robbery scene through the night after hours.

After twenty-eight days of shooting and a couple trips down to La Luz for pick up shots with an even smaller crew than we started with, we wrapped principle photography. In fact there was a week of filming where it was just me, the director John, and our cinematographer Richard Galli on set. We had to rig the boom up on a stand after pre-mixing the audio sounds. The director ran outside to perform a shadow gag, while the DP pressed record on the sound equipment and the camera, which he was operating. I was crying in character while slating for camera. It was a true labor of love.

NOW on to post-production, where we learned we were only twenty percent done with the movie the day we wrapped shooting. Here came the hard part, staying dedicated to having a completed movie. John, single handedly, edited "Home Sweet Home", and I continue to marvel at his talent. Most directors have a hard time seeing outside their project, but he was able to piece together a stellar movie. After he cut the film, I sat down with him, and together we went through the movie with what John likes to call "the iron fist" and started cutting everything and anything that wasn't absolutely needed for the story. We called up some dear friends and asked them to come over and watch the first edit and give us HONEST notes. Once the film was in a solid place we hired a sound designer and finally got to pass the film off to someone else, and breathe for a minute.

Through a miraculous turn of events I attended a Women in Film luncheon where I met Bridget Jurgens and Jen Sparks from Dog and Pony Creative, a fabulous poster company. These women have now become my dear friends, mentors, and creators of our AWARD winning posters for "Home Sweet Home." Bridget took precious time out of her schedule, spending hours with me going over the importance of marketing for a movie, and putting her advice into action, I wrote press releases to horror website to gain exposure for the film.

We flew the Rick Galli, the cinematographer out to LA. The director and Rick sat down in our dining room (converted into an office space) with a program they had access to and color corrected the film themselves. Once sound design was complete, and the movie was in the best place we could get it at. We submitted to over fifteen festivals, and premiered at the Albuquerque Film Festival, where we took home Audience Choice Award and Best Horror Film. Being so well received by the audience, our confidence grew and we knew that we did in fact have something special here.

The press releases brought phone calls from sales reps, and this began the process of sending out screeners to secure our rep. It was very important for John and me to find an agent that we really connected with, and who truly believed in our movie. After speaking with Ryan and Jonny from Instrum International, we felt we had met our guys. They were honest and genuine, and after meeting them in person we signed contracts to team up and bring "Home Sweet Home" to the public. And that's exactly what they did! This business partnership has evolved into a friendship, and they are now developing our next movie with us. The film industry really is all about relationships that you must nurture and protect with your life. All who are a part of "Home Sweet Home" truly ARE friends and family.

American Film Market was just a few months away, and with suggestions from Instrum, we made some tweaks to the film. John continued to fine tune it and prepare it for market.

With dedicated sales reps, a killer poster art, and a beautifully shot, skillfully acted, suspense driven film, we SOLD to Image Entertainment for US Distribution.

"Home Sweet Home" became available in

- TARGET
- WAL-MART
- AMAZON
- iTUNES
- BEST BUY
- NETFLIX

So to wrap it all up "JUST DO IT"!!!!

And please enjoy the MOVIE!

25. Your Job is Never Done

My partner and I recently delivered our second feature film to our distribution company, and boy did it feel good to pass it off to someone else. Our sleepless nights were over . . . for a moment.

When I was telling this exciting news to a friend, he asked, "So is your job done now? Are you guys finished with this film?"

I laughed and said, "Our job is never done."

Yes the hard drive containing all our work for the past year and half has been passed off, but as independent filmmakers our job is never done. Now on to the next phase: marketing our film. Once we get a release date, our job will be to tell people to go see our film and sending out press releases to bloggers and websites to help spread the word.

Even though the distribution company will put money into marketing the film, no one will work as hard as we will to spread the word, fill movie theaters and sell out DVDs.

Our first feature film, "Home Sweet Home" was released June of 2013. To this day we are STILL out there spreading the word, because, it's our movie and ultimately up to us to be its biggest champion. You cannot rely on anyone else to do it for you.

I bumped into Bryan Stumpf, who writes reviews for the horror website "The Slaughtered Bird," at a premier the other night. He mentioned that he wanted to see "Home Sweet Home" and I jumped at the opportunity to have him review it. I personally delivered to him the only copy we had left.

It was worth it. The review was the best we have ever received, and this comes a year and half after the film was released.

This is one of the reasons it is so important to be fully and completely passionate about the project you decide to invest your time into, because you will be working with it, well, forever!

It's also important to work with a team that is equally passionate about the project, so that you know everyone involved will be right alongside you spreading the word about the film.

The marketplace is flooded with films, and it's easy to get lost in the shuffle. As DVDs are becoming obsolete, and VOD is taking over, the hustle required for an indie filmmaker grows even greater.

But your dedication, drive, and pure passion will push you through the endless hours of promotion. And let's face it; if you aren't passionate about your film, then you won't put in the hours it takes to gain the awareness of the masses. And in turn no one will ever know about your film.

So my advice to indie filmmakers is be your project's biggest fan, because your job is never done.

FINANCING/DISTRIBUTION

26. Why Your Film Needs a Professional Poster

The most important part of your budget for a film is THE POSTER!

I am telling you the truth; there is no reason or excuse to skimp on a professional poster. Key Art is the calling card for your movie. It is the first thing the distribution company and your audience will see; it's what grabs their attention. Next comes the trailer. If you hook them with a great poster, then you will get the opportunity to show your trailer, and LAST they will watch your movie. So your poster is the most important part of your film.

I've had many conversations about this with other filmmakers and I've been surprised to learn that indie filmmakers are not aware of this extremely important part of the process of making a movie. Nor do they want to spend the money on it. Industry professionals know the difference between a poster made by professionals and those made by your friends.

I'm sure your friend is a good artist. They can paint, they can draw, but they can't make you the movie poster your film deserves. If you wanted to build a house you probably wouldn't have your friend come over and do it just because they built a birdhouse once. You would hire the person who knows how to do the job right, a professional. And don't even get me started on saying you can do it yourself . . . unless you run a professional and successful poster company.

A professional company knows what's selling in the market place and educated in what distribution companies are looking for and what box stores want. A professional poster company will help you create a poster that is not only sleek and catching, but that delivers your film at a glance. That is what you are paying for. It's worth it.

After completing my first feature film, "Home Sweet Home" I met "Dog and Pony Creative" run by Bridget Jurgens and Jen Sparks. I explained to them that numerous film festivals had rejected us and I was at a loss for where to go next with our movie. They encouraged me to make a killer poster to grab people's attention. After perusing their website, and getting to know them, I knew they were the company to team up with. I hired them.

The result is now an award winning poster that also got us our sales agents and caught the attention of our future distributor.

At the American Film Market our sales reps were sitting with Image Entertainment as they flipped through their book of films for sale. They stopped at our poster and said "That one, do we get this poster if we buy this film?"

Our sales reps confirmed that we owned the rights to the key art. That is when Image Entertainment requested a copy of our screener. If our poster hadn't been so well put together, the company would have looked right past it, and never given our film a second glance.

The movie went on to do extremely well in the market place, and I know a huge factor is how eye catching the poster is. In fact, I visited a local video store in California one day to see how our film was doing, and the man behind the counter said we were checked out non-stop. "Your cover grabs people, and that's why it's still in the new release section a month after its arrival."

In the entertainment world today most films go straight to video on demand or streaming platforms. The only thing your audience has a chance to see is your poster. All that stands between your film and an audience is a PICTURE! Whether you are self-distributing or want to get picked up by a distribution company, you'd better have the best poster that money and talent can buy.

The moment you have a budget to make a film, the first thing you need to do is set aside money to hire a professional poster company. Your movie won't miss those dollars, but your poster will.

You can have the most amazing movie in the world, but if your poster isn't high quality, than it doesn't matter cause chances are no one will ever see it.

27. From Big Budget to No Budget: The Joys of Indie Filmmaking

I recently returned home from the New Mexico desert where I was shooting a super micro budget film with a team of four, including myself. I was surprised by how many people asked me, "Why did you make this movie?" "Do you have a distribution deal?" "Why would you make a no budget film, after you just made a big budget film?"

Frankly I was a bit surprised by how many people asked me these questions. I am a filmmaker; it is my heart, my soul, and my passion to tell stories. I need creativity, like I need air to breathe. It isn't about the bottom line; it is about my pure need to create.

Honestly if you don't truly love the creative process of making a movie, then this business is not for you. It is a very small percentage of producers, writers, actors, and directors who earn a living off of making their own movies.

For me it was actually extremely refreshing to go from the high intensity stress of making a movie with investors' money, dealing with star talent, and running a forty-five-person crew, to being out in the middle of nowhere with a couple of my friends, just having fun. Every day we woke up, drank coffee, went over the script, and headed out to location to shoot, sometimes six scenes in one day! It was a blast. It felt like I was returning to my roots. Making movie magic for fun, without any expectations of what will happen when the movie is complete. There is no guarantee for independent films anyway, correction, there is no guarantee for any film, PERIOD!

With all the tools available to filmmakers today, there is no reason people can't be making their own films all the time. Even if you're doing it just to learn, which you should be, it's worth it to pick up a camera, grab some friends and make something. It will also give you the insight into whether you want to truly be in this business or not. Because if you don't want to make no budget films, just for fun, to be creative with your friends, then the chances of you surviving this business are slim to none.

No one asks a painter, "Why did you paint that painting?"

And if they do it's probably because they wanted to know the inspiration behind the artwork. Be inspired to tell stories, and don't be afraid to ask yourself, "Why am I not making a movie?"

Follow "At Your Own Risk" via our website: atyourownriskmovie.com

Instagram: atyour_ownrisk

Twitter: @atyour_ownrisk

28. Passion vs. Profit

Passion is an all-consuming feeling! Passion is the driving force behind the people who will truly go on to succeed. Because it wasn't economic success they were after, it was the feeding of their souls in creating their hearts' desire.

I meet a lot of industry people who say they want to make films because they love doing it, then I hear a counter balance with how much money people think they will make.

My dear friend and collaborator on "Your Pizza Adventure," Raquel Cantu, and I had a long conversation about this the other day. I felt compelled to take inventory of where my true desire lay with the outcome of my projects. Of course we all want to make money, no question about that, but if our focus and desire isn't in the right place we will falter along the path to success. When the roadblocks start popping up, it must be pure passion that keeps you knocking them down. And since monetizing something is the hardest thing for an artist to do, money alone will never sustain your drive to follow through to the end.

Raquel and I were reminiscing about our first feature film and how the group had never discussed money or had any expectations of where the film would go. We honestly just hoped our friends and family would see it, and that maybe it would be a good calling card for our next film. And because we had no insane expectation, all along the way we got more excited as better and better things kept happening! Instead of being disappointed all the time, we were amazed at how all the pieces came together. We call our movie "The little movie that could." It just kept going and going. We won in our hearts just because "Home Sweet Home" was made and then we won again when the movie was sold. Because we had no real agenda at the beginning of the process, we were blown away by the end result and felt so blessed that our little movie is now sitting on the shelves of Wal-Mart! Itis so important for love and passion to be the main focus. Monetizing can take a REALLY long time. If you're waiting for your pocket book to get filled, you'll be robbed of the joy that is the process of creating the project.

As I sift through memories of creating projects, I feel overwhelmed with love. I truly love it. It is my hearts' desire. I believe that is the reason everything I put my mind to accomplishing has come to fruition.

Our app team is a big believer in celebrating every small accomplishment. Giving yourself little victories along the way will keep you sane and fulfilled. This helped us get through over a year and a half of writing, shooting, and editing. Only four of us made this project and we would shoot for twelve-hour days, on our own dime, with no guarantee of financial gain. It was important for us to celebrate each step along the way. It kept us connected as a group, excited about the project, and kept our morale high as we crossed each new finish line. I highly recommend doing this on your projects. Celebrate each win!

Creating the app game was so rewarding that I don't think money will feel as good as it felt the first time we actually played the game on the iPhone. To see our vision come to life in a real way; our invention a reality-THAT was our WIN!

While we were knee deep in the process of creating the app, I was working a side job. I would wake up with the crew at seven am and shoot all day, and then as the sun was setting, I'd run home to put on my apron and waitress until two am. I did this for the four months of shooting and it still amazes me that somehow I managed to sustain this crazy work schedule. But I can honestly say that my passion was driving me forward and I was so in love with what we were doing that my happiness sustained me through my sleep deprivation. If you love what you do you will never work a day in your life. Most artists need to have side jobs but as long as you are doing what you love on the other side, hope will thrive and your heart will be full.

I admire my fellow teammates at Black Sheperd Productions, creators of the web series, "Flock." They embody loving what you do and finding the time to do it. We shot that show on the weekends over the course of a full year! Now that is dedication! This whole team worked around their crazy work schedules to complete this incredible show. Juggling full time jobs and financial difficulties we still found a way to make this project come to life and see it through to completion.

After spending ten years struggling in Los Angeles as an actor, I moved to New Mexico with intent to rediscover who I was and what I wanted to do with my life. My grip on the desire to be an actor was so tight and I had such tunnel vision that I couldn't see outside of the box I had accidentally created. I had built imaginary walls around myself and I had no idea how to climb out. I went to Albuquerque to break the mold I had created and there I discovered what I truly desired.

Like air we need to breathe, I had to be a creative person. Regardless of money, I was pursuing what I truly desired. It didn't matter if I struggled forever, as long as I was doing what I loved to do! Now my walls were torn down, my hands open to all opportunities. I was outside of my box.

It required removal from my old world to discover a brave new world that I wanted to create for myself. No longer waiting for people to choose me, I chose myself!

Many people battle it out to complete their movie and make money so that they can "live the dream." Let me fill you in on a secret: the act of pursuing your dream IS living the dream. It isn't something that comes later. It is something that is.

Find your passion and then go after it with all your might. If you really love something you will find a way to do it; no excuses, no distractions. Find a group of people who want to swim in your pool, and dive in headfirst. I once read that Lena Dunham, creator of the show "Girls," worked a day job and then came home and wrote all night long. If you want something bad enough you will find the time and the love of doing it will get you through the hard times. Money doesn't feed your soul, dreaming does. And the money will come, but first there has to be passion and motivation. Talent and hard work will win out in the end! And no matter what happens, no one can ever take away your project, your creation. This value in your life is far above gold and silver!

Passion vs. Profit. Which one are you trying to get? If it's not out of passion I encourage you to step back and reevaluate, because if you are seeking monetary gain you may make the wrong choices for your project and find yourself disappointed. If you make decisions based on your passion, chances are if you love it, others will love it too.

And when money does come, then that's just the extra scrumptious icing on the very delicious cake you already made!

29. Filmmakers, Are You Ready for an Investor's Money?

Are you ready for an investor's money?

So I hear you have a great idea, but you're wondering, "How do I pay for that great idea?" This leads you to looking for investors to fund that amazing idea of yours. But here comes the really BIG question we have all heard a million times, "What have you done?"

This question used to drive me crazy. I kept thinking I know I can execute my incredible concept if someone would just believe in me and hand over a pile of cash to bring my vision to life. How do you make something without money? But now, after years of funding my own projects, I fully understand the significance of this question. Everyone has a great idea, but not everyone can or will follow through from concept to completion. In fact, I have discovered it is better to practice on your own ideas with your own money first. I grasp the magnitude of needing to witness an artist execute a project from begin to end before someone is willing to invest in her work.

The money will come, but first you must prove your abilities and skills. The process of making a feature film is intense, mind boggling, and straight up HARD WORK! When we began the journey of making "Home Sweet Home" I had no idea what I was getting myself into. Just when you think your job is done, boom, there are a million more things to do. And the entire process took over two and half years. Creating is no easy task, and I'm thankful I didn't have the pressure of outsiders' money on my shoulders along with all the other demands looming over me. We were really just learning how to figure it all out!

Now that we have established ourselves as a filmmaking team with great ideas, capable of executing them, and then going on to sell them; the opportunities are starting to arise where people feel confident to invest in us. In fact, people who said they would never invest in projects, now, three years later with a feature film on the shelves of major stores and an app game available on the App Store, those same people are coming out of the woodwork ready to invest in our projects.

When someone invests in an idea, they are really investing in the promise of the people who will make that idea a reality.

When we completed our second feature film titled "Catching Faith," funded by investors, the pressure was heavy. You can't make mistakes; there is no room for that when you spend other people's money. Make all your mistakes with your own money, so that when those checks come in from investors, you know how to best use the money, and you know your team can deliver the goods.

Go out there and make your calling card, which demonstrates your talent, abilities and determination. Learn, fail, fall down, get up, and learn again, all on your own accord. Find a group of like-minded friends (preferably with different skills than you), buy a camera (or use your phone camera) and get out there on the streets and start doing it! Only then are you ready to take other parties' hard earned money, because the worst thing that could happen is to not be ready, and ruin your chance of future investments. You can only make a first impression once!

Don't road block yourself with all the excuses-I don't have the perfect camera, I don't have the right lights (or any at all), I don't have enough crew members, If you prove you have what it takes to complete a marvelous project, then you have something to show for yourself when the question arises, "What have you done?" And a smart savvy investor will know that with their funding you will be able to make something even better.

You will feel confident and comfortable bringing in that investor, because you know how the entire process works from the brilliant idea, to shooting it, editing it, marketing it, selling it and so much more that goes into the completion of a Great Idea!

Don't waste your precious time waiting for funding, because no one wants to get involved in something until they see "What you have done." And honestly that's a good thing! You don't want the responsibility of other people's money until you know you CAN bring the project to the finish line! Prove yourself first and everything will follow!

30. Sold!

My feature film "Home Sweet Home" sold at the America Film Market to Image Entertainment. The exciting news came on the last day of the market, and now I must share how such a little indie film got bought by such a big company.

Before we even took meetings with a sales rep, we had:

1.   A Great Title
2.   A Great Tag Line
3.   A Great Poster
4.   A Great Product

Of course, in every business endeavor timing is key to everything. What really sold our movie was the marketing materials. We had everything a distribution company needed to make it an easy sell.

I am writing my next film with all these things in mind ahead of time. I strongly encourage any other filmmaker out there to do the same.

31. We Made an APP Game; "Your Pizza Adventure" has Arrived!

I have been referencing this app game in so many of my previous articles, that I'm thrilled to announce its officially launched on the App Store and I want to share the journey with you. I'm excited to give a realistic account of the time, effort and money it took to complete this unique live action game.

Our team, which consisted of four filmmakers and one programmer, spent two years completing this project. It has been a labor of love from day one. A couple of years ago some of my fellow teammates and me drove from Los Angeles to New Mexico where we were shooting our feature film "Home Sweet Home." I recommend road trips because I find the best ideas come out on the drive. As we were driving through the desert late at night the conversation turned to our love for "choose your own adventure" books from our childhood. We thought how exciting it would be to create something similar for a new generation: a movie where the audience could choose and change the course of the story. Everything from a horror movie (which weapon does the victim pick up to defend themselves) or a romantic story (what does the girl say on her date and how would that affect what happens next.) We struggled with what kind of platform could host an interactive movie. We initially thought maybe we could turn it into a web series, then realized there was no way to monetize it. So we put the idea on the back burner and finished filming our movie.

There was a cold snap in New Mexico while we were shooting our film and we had to put the cast and crew up at a neighbor's house because there was no running water on the property where we were shooting. It turned out that the son of the woman's house we were staying at was an app programmer. After we finished the film he contacted my husband John and I about shooting an app idea he had wanted to make. That idea never came to fruition, but put a light bulb on in our brains that maybe we could turn our movie-game idea into an app. We called the programmer and he said it was completely possible to make a live action app game. Many things we think are curses, such as losing running water, can become a blessing.

The four of us–John Graham, Raquel Cantu, Andrew Maiorano and me – gathered together in our living room and started out on an insane, mind-boggling, journey to figure out how to make our idea a reality. We began with poster boards; creating spider webs of where the story split off into different directions. It was a huge challenge to convert these story maps into script form but we invented a numbering system and jumped into shooting on the streets around our houses. After giving the script to our friend Jason Dibler to play the zombie, he called us immediately loving the idea: "I've always wanted to tell the character in a movie to go out the front door not up the stairs, and now the audience can."

The four of us pitched in money to buy costumes, food, props and any other odds and ends we might need along the way. We alternated from holding the camera and boom, to keeping track of the decision points and soon began pulling our hair out trying to figure out how to shoot this beast. With complete satisfaction and exhaustion four months later we finished filming every pathway. It was like shooting three feature films at the same time.

The challenges were far from over. Next we moved into the editing room. Because it was a non-linear story line we used the numbering system to track where each video went depending on what the audience chose at that moment. John and I turned our apartment into an office space, where our team would meet every day in the beginning to write and then edit once we entered into post-production

Throughout this process people told us that what we were doing was impossible. That technology wasn't ready. The amount of videos would crash the phones or take too long to load. Since no one had seen this done before it must, therefore, be impossible to do. The naysayers gave us courage actually. We kept saying we'll prove them wrong and to our satisfaction we did.

I was recently talking to a friend and asked him what he thought the next big thing in entertainment was. He paused and said, "I don't know. I think people make what the next big thing is." I beamed at his response; it reminded me of what I had been working on for two years. We didn't wait for someone to give us permission to create something outside the box, or wait till it was a big hit; we gave ourselves permission to make up our own rules.

Once all the videos had been edited it was time for the programmer to build the game. It was his job to take the finished videos–each of which was like a little short film that had been edited, sound designed and color corrected–and bundle them together into a playable app.

Just when we were ready to pass the videos to our programmer he, for personal reasons, had to pull out of the project. We were devastated by this turn of events. After the four of us had put our lives on hold and spent a year writing, shooting and editing, it felt like all hope was lost. With no money to pay for a programmer and so many people already telling us we were wasting our time, our spirits were crushed.

Luckily we didn't give up and kept trucking forward contacting everyone we knew. By the grace of God we were introduced to an incredible programmer, Noah Karrer, who believed in the project and came on board as our partner. A friend of mine from New Mexico referred us to this man. One never knows how the choices we make or the people we encounter will play a life saving role in our lives. That's why I always say be kind; the film industry is a small town, be open to all opportunities.

Noah came to our house for a meeting and we handed him a bunch of papers with numbers strung together, of a hundred and fifty different decision points and a hard drive with three hundred videos all labeled with our crazy numbering system. This talented man took all this and turned it into an interactive game.

Apple approved our game and it runs smoothly and is available to the whole world. This proves that nothing is impossible. The key is to not give up, keep pushing through the roadblocks. We never know how the outcome will look. Just when I think something is set in stone it turns into clay and transforms.

I hope this story inspires other entrepreneurs to never give up on their dreams. It might feel impossible in the moment, but if the project is worth it and it's important to you, you will do it. I can't stress enough how important it is that you LOVE LOVE LOVE the project your investing your time, money, and heart into. Nothing happens overnight.

I was asked to speak at a high school about making our app game. One of the questions proposed to me was: "What genre movie do you recommend I make?" My response was, "Whatever genre you love, because if you love what you are making, chances are the audience will love it to."

If you love it, then you won't give up when the going gets rough. We love horror movies, so we made a horror movie. We love silly goofy funny outrageous comedy so we made that kind of Movie App Game. You must adore your own work first because you could go around a room full of people and ask them what is "*good*" and you will get a different answer from each one of them, so do what is "*good*" for you.

I am a huge fan of Seth Godin's blog. On his website it says "Go Make Something Happen." I am proud of my friends and teammates who MADE something happen. In the face of adversity, we didn't give up, we persevered, shocking even ourselves with our bravery.

Is there something you would love to Make Happen*?*

DO IT- Go forth and live the life you always wanted! And in the meantime please play my game.

Conclusion

What it means to ME to be a Ms. In The Biz

And this goes for all the Mr.'s out there too

#1. A Ms. in the Biz does not complain about the problems she sees in the film industry towards women, no way, because she doesn't have time to complain. She is too busy solving the problem. She is being the change she wants to see in the world.

#2. A Ms. in the Biz is not afraid to stand up for what she believes is best for a project. She is not scared to speak her mind, even if it isn't the most popular opinion in the room. She believes her voice is valuable and worthy to be heard.

#3. A Ms. in the Biz surrounds herself with men who champion women, and respect them as partners. They find and work men who are excited to share the head of the table with them.

#4. A Ms. in the biz sends the ladder down to the women on the next rung. She does not believe that there is only room for a couple of women at the top; she believes there is an unlimited amount of space for all her fellow female filmmakers.

#5. A Ms. in the Biz hires and champions women. She understands that men are not against us, but not necessarily always thinking about us. Therefore, it is her responsibility to find all the applications from women crew and hire them when it is the best fit for the project.

#6. A Ms. in the Biz makes sure the script she is producing has strong positive female characters. Something the next generation can look up to.

#7. A Ms. in the Biz nurtures and mentors younger female filmmakers, so that soon there will be no inequality between men and women in Hollywood.

#8. A Ms. in the Biz leads by example, treating everyone on her set with respect and kindness, setting the environment for everyone to follow. She believes that everyone involved in the film is important and valuable.

Don't wait for someone else to make your dreams happen, make them happen yourself.

Go out there and make movies, tell stories, and surround yourself with the best of the best!

You can continue to follow my career via the pages below:

- Facebook
  https://www.facebook.com/alexandra.boylan1
- Instagram @alexandraboylan
- Twitter @aboylan4

FINAL THOUGHTS

Rising Together:

There is a huge need for women to ban together to create projects in the entertainment industry. There is a scary low number of females behind the camera. One of the reasons this may be is because woman tend to be more competitive and jealous than men are. Men help each other in the work place and tend to rise together. If women banned together instead of tearing each other apart, we may very well see a rise in female filmmakers.

We need more women in power positions, so the ladies are calling the shots. We must encourage each other to hire women in jobs that might normally go to a man. When women are in the position of hiring, they can choose to hire women and they must choose to hire women, then we will see more females taking jobs behind the camera.

And yet, men can be the best allies for women, and great partners. When a woman and a man equally work together on a project, incredible results are born.

When women have an equal place at the table, alongside the men, we are finally revolutionizing the future.

Women accounted for just sixteen percent of all the directors, executive producers, producers, writers, cinematographers, and editors who worked on the top-grossing two hundred and fifty domestic films of 2013, and were just twenty-eight percent of all off screen talent on broadcast television programs during the 2012-13 primetime season.

(Found from "Fact Sheet: The Women's Leadership Gap" by Judith Warner.

It is no surprise to anyone that the film industry is run by men, it's a man's club, and the only way to transform this, is for more women to stand up and start creating projects.

Women can't just wait to be hired, women need to be the creators of the project, so they can control who is being hired. Seems like common sense right? So why is it that there is still such a small percentage of females behind the camera?

As we see more and more strong female players such as Tina Fey, Mindy Keling, Angelina Jolie, we feel encouraged that there is a shift happening.

Is Angelina breaking breaking the glass ceiling for female directors? It needs to be done; we need more Kathrine Bigalows out there, to create room for more of us to wiggle ourselves into any available space.

Are woman making the list? When execs put out the call for a list of directors to Shepard a film, are there even women names on the list? There is a good chance, they aren't even making the initial conversation, so then how on earth would they ever get a job?

How do we get more point of views from female perspectives? We need to add some ladies to the list! That would at least be a start. We need females sitting next to men in the creating room.

Women need to be brave and take initiative in their own career, stop waiting for permission to do something, give yourself permission and begin it.

"It's now estimated that, at the current rate of change, it will take until 2085 for women to reach parity with men in leadership roles in our country." Judith Warner.

So females, and males need to get hustling on changing the way things are done, decided, and breach the gender gap.

If we work together we can create this change, we are all so desperate to see in the world!

Not only do women need to create projects, and put themselves in the power positions, but when a woman gets in that position they need to hire more womn.

Lets all rise together and take action.

Create your own Career, in Hollywood.

Printed in Great Britain
by Amazon